That's Me
In the Corner

Coming Out as An Atheist
on Facebook

Jason D. Eden

ISBN-10: 1495212785
ISBN-13: 978-1495212789

DEDICATION

Dedicated to all of the heroes of reason and truth who have sacrificed jobs, friendships, family relationships, and sometimes even their lives in a simple attempt to seek out and believe what is actually true.

CONTENTS

CONTENTS CONTINUED

PREFACE (PART 1)

What if being honest meant losing things that were dear to you?

- Your job?
- Your standing in the community?
- Your friendships?
- Your family relationships?
- Your marriage?

Would you have the ability to maintain a lie if you thought it was mostly harmless in order to keep these things in your life in place? I suspect many of you reading this already do. Some of you reject the authority of the Bible as I do, for the same reasons, or at least have serious questions about it. However, you still publicly proclaim that it is the "inspired word of God" and sincerely hope that no one challenges you on it.

I believe the questions you have to ask yourself are:

- At what point of harm does a lie become too great to maintain, regardless of the cost?
- At what point does bigotry against homosexuals, women, people who don't believe the same things you do, and people of other nations and races become untenable for you, even if it is endorsed by your holy writings?
- At what point does the unconscionable act of lying about science in order to indoctrinate your children start to cause real harm both to them and to the scientific progress of humanity in general?
- At what point does the money spent on lavish cathedrals, massive salaries, enormous mansions, and private jets for ministers and their self-serving ministries start to weigh on your conscience when children around the world die every day from lack of food, water, and basic sanitation?
- At what point should people who refuse medical treatment for their sick children based on "the power of prayer" - which has been proven time and time again to be ineffective - lose the right to make those decisions for their kids?

If belief in the supernatural were truly harmless, I'd have no problem maintaining the lie. Unfortunately, believing a lie is never really truly harmless, and it affects real-life decisions: sometimes as small as a hiring manager choosing a lesser-qualified candidate based on bigotry, sometimes as large as a national leader seeing himself as a fulfillment of some dark end-times prophecy. Truth matters, it turns out, and it can matter a lot.

For many of us embedded in our religious communities, however, the cost of saying "the emperor has no clothes" comes at a steep price. Full-time clergy or religious business leaders who have come to the realization that their faith is a sham risk financial hardship for their families if they come clean to their followers or customers. Religious people in the community will almost certainly talk about "that poor family with the atheist mom/dad" and put them on various prayer lists (gossip chains). If most of your friendships, family relationships, and even your marriage are based on a common set of beliefs, you risk losing it all. When reading through profiles of other members of The Clergy Project, it appears that the divorce rate for clergy who dare speak honestly about their doubts or lack of faith is amazingly high, with marriage survival being the exception rather than the rule.

Thus, I have a lot of sympathy those of you who, for whatever reason, can't let yourselves follow truth wherever it leads. I get the struggle. I understand the potential social costs and the nearly certain loss of important relationships. I do not ask you to follow me on my public truth journey - not yet. The request I have for you is to find ways to help those of us for whom the cost of living a lie has become too high:

- Continue being our friends and lean into that relationship just a little bit more.
- Be a listening ear and a shoulder to cry on when we need it.
- Be a place of refuge in our lives.
- Perhaps consider direct financial assistance if needed.
- Support us - even if just privately - in our fight for truth and honesty, because in the end, we're fighting also for your right to be honest with the world about who you really are.

Someday, maybe, you'll get to add your voice to the growing chorus of non-belief without fear of losing those things that matter most. That hope, friends, is why this book exists.

(PREFACE PART 2)
A NOTE FROM MY CHRISTIAN WIFE

I have known my husband for more than 20 years now and witnessed first-hand his spiritual and religious journey over that time period. It is safe to say no one knows him better than I do.

We met at the beginning of our college years. I can attest to the fact that Jason was a strong Christian. He believed in God, in the death and resurrection of Christ, and lived his life as reflection of these truths. He believed in the purpose and mission of the church and was very active in ministry before, during and after college. Jason was bothered by the reality that others in the world did not believe, and as he approaches many matters in life, he approached his religion from primarily an intellectual standpoint. It's part of who he is. He believed that if he could logically show others evidence for the existence of God, unbelievers would be able to believe. Jason studied the Bible thoroughly for many years and spent more time and effort studying, learning, and examining scripture than many full time ministers and leaders of the church.

Jason believed in God, studied and believed God's word, and always made time to be involved in church work. Jason was always willing to share his faith and discuss questions surrounding the Bible with both believers and non-believers. Jason was always interested in talking to those who were struggling with their faith, as well as those who said they wanted to believe but just had tough questions. Jason was willing and able to do what many Christians are not, which was to have an honest conversation with non-believers and let them express the specific questions and hang-ups that kept them from believing. Jason and I attended and were involved with "seeker sensitive" churches for more than a decade. Jason was passionate about making God accessible to non-religious folks who were looking for something more. When witnessing to non-believers, rather than telling the person that they just had to believe and have faith, he was willing and very able to discuss with them from an intellectual, factual and evidence-based standpoint why God is real and the Bible is true.

Some people who don't know Jason hear his story of deconversion and are quick to say that he was never a Christian in the first place. If choosing Jesus is a choice, it is a choice that Jason made before I met him, and lived out with the best of his abilities for more than two decades. Saying that Jason was never a Christian seems to be a quick and easy way for believers to dismiss his story. However, I have yet to personally hear from anyone who really knew Jason during those two decades who could honestly say that Jason's faith was not genuine, true, or a integral part of his life.

As explained more thoroughly in the pages of his book, Jason left his faith because science progressed in recent years and provided a plausible explanation for life and the physical universe to have come to be without God's presence. Unfortunately, Christian apologetics has not kept up with defending the faith in light of scientific findings over the past decade. Jason explores the possibility of life coming into existence without the hand of a Creator. He explains some elements of morality and human behavior and why people can choose to behave ethically and morally for reasons other than the threat of Hell. Jason's book is compelling and thought provoking as it outlines and discusses some very tough questions regarding the Christian faith. Some are questions that Christians may have but are afraid to ask or ponder. Some are questions that non-believers have that keep them from accepting God.

There were some Christians who read Jason's Facebook posts, engaged with Jason and defended their views. Some doomed Jason to Hell and promptly unfriended him. Some didn't engage in a discussion, but simply said he should have more faith. And some who at first seemed interested in the topics Jason discussed ultimately did not respond. Jason presents tough questions that require research and contemplation. There are no quick and easy answers. If there were, defenders of the faith would have already laid these questions to rest on Facebook.

The book does not necessarily offer a final resolution of these issues. Jason is being honest when he says he is open to being wrong. He always has been open to further discussion of most any topic, and it's one of his more endearing qualities as a husband. Perhaps a Christian reading this book can provide my husband with new insights – something he has not yet considered. I really hope that is the outcome of this book, rather than instant rejection of Jason's thoughts and questions from the Christian community.

I accepted Christ many years ago, and despite Jason's book and the scientific findings that drew him away from faith, I still choose to believe in the existence of God and in the death and resurrection of Christ. I hope that Christian apologists can look at current scientific findings and continue to defend the existence of a Creator. To think that, as Christians, we shouldn't have to prove anything or defend our beliefs is shortsighted. Christians have always needed to defend their beliefs, and this book should provide a challenge to do so rather than be viewed as some scary untouchable ideas that shouldn't be acknowledged.

In my opinion, it is not our call as Christians to simply join the church club and only surround ourselves with others in the faith. We are here to interact with and be involved with those of no faith or differing faiths, and to be prepared to defend our faith and perhaps persuade others to believe in the God of the Bible. If God is all-knowing, all-powerful, and all-loving, then surely it is okay to seek understanding and answers to difficult questions.

Melynda Eden

FOREWORD

I met Jason Eden when he joined The Clergy Project in August, 2013. The Clergy Project (TCP) is an online support group of more than 500 active and former clergy from various faiths come together to share the struggles of being a non-believer in a context where your life, community, and for our actives, your livelihood are wrapped up in a context of faith in the supernatural. As Jason articulated in the preface of this book, it is a challenging position to be in.

Before joining TCP, the only person Jason had been able to talk to about his departure from faith was his wife. Based on the volume of posts and interactions Jason engaged in during his first couple of months, she probably deserves some kind of award for having handled all of that pent up energy and cognitive dissonance. :) Jason was not an active clergy at the time due to personal circumstances, but his life was still very enmeshed in a faith identity that he no longer believed to be valid.

As it is with all of our members, it was a privilege to watch him process his conflicting feelings, survey his situation, and develop strategies with the support and input from many others in TCP who had gone down this road before. One of his early posts was titled "What I Would Say (in Public) if I Thought I Could." After getting feedback from other TCP members, he used these initial thoughts to come out to a small group of friends and family. Over time, that group broadened, and we at TCP got to walk with Jason every step of the way. He would post his fears, TCP would validate them and provide strategic advice. He would post ideas and phrasings, ask for suggestions, and TCP would help him phrase things for greatest clarity and effect. We were there with him every step of the way, encouraging him, cheering for him, and helping him navigate the many land mines that await nearly anyone who chooses to come clean with their nonbelief.

I also had the privilege of being one of Jason's Facebook friends, and thus got to witness first-hand his "coming out" posts and the ensuing discussions. From our personal interactions, I already had a sense of Jason's productivity, intelligence, integrity, and sensitivity. Watching it all on display in the context of emotionally charged and sometimes hostile situations was a lot of fun. I am very glad Jason chose to make that part of his journey public through this book. I suspect there are many, many people who are not friends with Jason on Facebook who will find his coming out experience to be of tremendous value.

Terry Plank
Board President, The Clergy Project (http://ClergyProject.org)
Board of Directors, The Humanist Society (http://Humanist-Society.org)

INTRODUCTION

I was saved[1] during Vacation Bible School in 1984 at the age of nine. For me, it was a no-brainer: reject Jesus and go to Hell, or accept him and go to Heaven. Never questioning the validity of my small-church Southern Baptist teachings, I made the decision to accept Jesus into my heart and was baptized shortly thereafter.

In my early teens I "surrendered into the ministry" and began preaching. I had a love of public speaking and a sincere heart for making people's lives better. I led Bible Study groups at my school and participated in them with adults when I was old enough to drive. I was a leader in our youth group evangelistic efforts, which included puppet, music, and mime (acting out religious story songs) ministries. I led See You At the Pole[2] and National Day of Prayer events. I unsuccessfully campaigned to allow prayer and religious teaching at my high school graduation. In my Southern Baptist college I participated in weekend Revival Teams[3] as either the speaker or the piano player. I took Old and New Testament classes for majors, as well as classes on evangelism (yes, three credit hours on how to read someone a tract and lead them through the prayer of salvation) and a full year of Biblical Hebrew. During college, I spent more than two years in part-time employment as a Youth Pastor for Antioch Baptist Church in Lebanon, Missouri.

---

[1] In Southern Baptist (and many other) religious traditions, salvation is defined as the moment you wholeheartedly say a prayer to consciously accept Jesus as your lord and savior. Other religious traditions define the experience as a progression rather than a specific moment.

[2] Occurs every fourth Wednesday in September. A voluntary gathering of students and faculty for scripture reading and prayer before school starts. http://en.wikipedia.org/wiki/See_You_at_the_Pole

[3] Revival Teams were a school-coordinated effort where a group of three students would perform a weekend revival service geared towards converting members of their youth group to the good news of the gospel.

After college, I served as a volunteer and then accepted an invitation to be a part-time Youth Pastor once again, this time as part of a non-denominational church in the Overland Park, Kansas area. In addition to my Youth Pastor role, I was also very active on the church's worship team (keyboard and voice) and participated in various leadership conferences either held at the church or at Willow Creek Community Church in the Chicago area.

When my wife and I moved to Springfield, Missouri a few years later, I served in leadership roles in an Evangelical Free church for a while, and later helped launch a church that eventually joined with the General Baptists. I primarily planned and led worship each week with a team of three extremely musically gifted teenagers, and would occasionally speak when the pastor when the pastor had other obligations.

A few years later my family moved to the Saint Louis area, and we began attending a large non-denominational church. After a few months I was ready to plug myself into their worship team and start exploring opportunities in their youth programs, but those things in my life came to a screeching halt when my then two-year-old son was diagnosed with autism. That journey consumed us for the next six years, so for the first time in my life since my early teens, I found myself an observer rather than a leader in church settings for an extended time period.

I include my church history in this book to answer the oft-heard objection "Well, you were never really a Christian to begin with." There was no one who was more sold on Jesus than I was. I had asked tough questions as a teen and found typical church answers wanting, but when I discovered philosophy and apologetics, I found the answers I needed and - I thought - my overall role in God's kingdom. I walked bravely into debates with atheists and agnostics, and for nearly 20 years. I felt more confident with each conversation as I challenged their misconceptions and assumptions about Christianity and pointed out how their belief system in many ways took more faith than my own. There were problems with the Bible - I knew them well - but I was a champion for Christianity who loved people and wanted them to experience the perfect love of God as I had. And I believe I was good at it too, if I do say so myself.

Time, however, was not kind to my positions. I boldly made predictions on what fossil records and quantum physics would discover, confident in the fact that my God had created it all and would leave the clues necessary to convince the skeptics of his existence. Evolution via natural selection would be proven false. It was impossible for matter and energy to simply appear out of nothing. My faith in the supernatural held these truths to be self-evident. And for a while, in a vacuum of definitive evidence, my arguments were hard to overcome. However, as more and more fossil evidence[4] started appearing that proved transitional forms did exist, my faith cracked. When genome mapping became possible and we discovered that there is just a 1-4%[5] difference (depending on how you look at it) in the genetic code between us and our closest animal relatives, my faith cracked a little more. When the knowledge that virtual particles and quantum foam had been unquestionably proven to exist hit my radar, I had proof that matter, in fact, *did* just appear from nothing[6], and it happens all the time. Neither God nor any other supernatural force was necessary to explain existence. My faith crumbled.

My first stop after that revelation was to go to my church for help. I attended a large mega-church, one that proclaims to be a "safe place to ask the big questions about God." I was sure that they would have someone on staff who could walk me through the information I had uncovered and show me why it did not mean my faith had been a lie. After one introductory conversation and a few email exchanges where I forwarded them my research, however, they informed me that they were *not* going to have these conversations with me. I was welcome to come back and talk when I was ready to discuss having a relationship with Jesus, but otherwise, they were not going to engage. I was absolutely floored. My questions and objections, I can only imagine, had been deemed so toxic - so outside the bounds of the questions they were encouraging others to ask - that they wouldn't even begin the conversation with me on any point. For me, that was when the scales fell from my eyes. If these guys with all of their available resources didn't have the answers, nobody did.

For the next couple of years I anguished over what had occurred and what it meant. Eventually I discovered Kenneth Daniels' amazing book *Why I Believed: Reflections of a Former Missionary*[7] and was captivated. I read

---

[4] http://en.wikipedia.org/wiki/Transitional_fossil
[5] Compare http://scitechdaily.com/bonobo-genome-completed-differs-from-humans-by-1-3-percent/ vs.
http://genome.cshlp.org/content/15/12/1746.long
[6] See http://www.pbs.org/wgbh/nova/blogs/physics/2012/10/quantum-foam-virtual-particles-and-other-curiosities/ and
http://www.livescribe.com/cgi-bin/WebObjects/LDApp.woa/wa/MLSOverviewPage?sid=D5Qt2728s5Bj
[7] http://www.amazon.com/Why-Believed-Reflections-Former-Missionary-ebook/dp/B003UNLMRY

page after page of nearly identical story lines, personal discovery, fears, and challenges. Reading his story inspired me to seek out additional stories, and one that I quickly found was Jerry Dewitt's book *Hope After Faith: An Ex-Pastor's Journey from Belief to Atheism*[8]. In his book, he described an organization known as The Clergy Project[9] (hereafter TCP) that existed as a support group for both active and former clergy who had given up belief in the supernatural. I immediately sought them out.

When I joined this group, I was able to read story after story of pain and loss - sometimes unimaginable loss - so I knew the stakes were as high as I suspected. I was also able to read and learn from their stories, as well as bounce ideas about my own coming out to a group in which many folks had been there, done that. It proved immensely valuable as a way to build up the courage to come clean with my friends and family (outside of my wife, who had been with me every step of the way) in the most strategic manner possible. Some TCP members told stories that were a triumph of human spirit and a heroic effort to replace what was lost by their honesty and desire to live authentic lives. Because of them, I was able to predict what might be lost far ahead of time, grieve over it, and put my replacements in place before I started coming out and fighting those battles. I am indebted to those who went before and showed me a way I could go with as little pain as possible. I love you guys and gals!

Even with all of this support, however, coming out as an atheist at 39 years old - having been such an active voice and defender of the Christian faith - was not an easy thing for me to do. I decided to do it in phases - first coming out to folks I knew were already atheists or agnostics, then broadening to small groups. I knew many of these coming out experiences would lead painful conversations, but this method allowed me to deal with those fires in small batches rather than one big explosion. I went through several rounds of "coming out" notifications and painful discussions until I finally went public with my deconversion in January 2014 via a Facebook announcement. I knew there would be many questions about my departure from faith, the reasons, and how I now addressed issues like cosmology and morality. Thus I decided to write a series of short posts, each one addressing one of the critical pieces of my departure and addressing the criticisms Christians would inevitably throw my way. I did this in part so that people I loved might come to understand what I was doing, and in part to give them a chance to show me flaws in my thinking or logic.

---

[8] http://www.amazon.com/Hope-after-Faith-Ex-Pastors-Journey-ebook/dp/B00C2TWWUI
[9] http://clergyproject.org/

Those Facebook posts (sometimes modified for clarity) and summaries of the relevant resulting conversations make up the bulk of this book. In no case have I attempted to change the meaning of what was said based on my personal opinion about what was written. In fact, the more critical and well-reasoned someone was, the more likely you are to see the conversation summarized and discussed.

You get to see the relevant and interesting questions and answers and decide for yourself if my journey is one of reason and honesty or a fool's folly in rebellion to God. I hope you find it a worthwhile experience.

ACKNOWLEDGMENTS

The thoughts detailed in this book were posted over a couple of weeks, however the thought processes that enabled them were formed over two decades of thought, discussion, and debate.

This book would not exist without the efforts and work of Christian apologist Norm Geisler, whose writings in defense of the faith probably kept me from leaving Christianity as a teenager. His work forced me to think very carefully about the universe in which I live and what it means for me to be here.

I would like to thank my ever-patient wife who, as a believer, prays for my soul yet still loves and accepts me in ways I sometimes struggle to comprehend. Many risk their marriages in order to be honest with the world about who they are. Not having to worry about that made and makes my life significantly less stressful.

I am thankful for all of my Facebook friends[10] who publicly engaged in my coming out series of conversations.

---

[10] In no particular order: Marc Pruter, Chris Huss, Nathan Perkins, Ken Thacker, John Arrasjid, Jennifer Adamson-O'Quinn, Stephen Ernst, Mason Lane, Todd Meador, Lisa Guinn, Eric Berglund, John Tuffin, Craig Loughrige, Richard Reilly, Nancy Johnson, Charles Lee, Erin Jackson Tucker, James F. Ross, Ashley Lavana, George Pradel, Chris Oestereich, Christopher Carpunky, Douglas Roberts, Teresa Dixon, Dennis Augustine, Sara Jo Plucker-Wright, Bill Griffith, Carolyn Hauser Wallace, Scott Olson, Chris Roberts, Mark Fei, Steve Bradshaw, Daniel Crider, Greg Finch, Bruce Morrill, David Krug, Bob King, Jodi Evans, Darrin Johnson, Brent Wynn, Judy Vanderpool Loper, John Carpenter, Rich Wellner, Joann Cogdill, Terry Plank, Stacy Thomas, Dustin Conrad, Brad Luzadder, Shawn Stewart, Deborah Joann Allen VanHam, and Ashley-Michelle Papon

Many people who followed my online coming out journey also reviewed my book and made helpful comments. I am grateful to them all, but I owe a special note of thanks to two individuals. First, I would like to thank my amazing editor, Molly Burkemper. Her eye for grammar and clarity of sentence structure is the best I have ever seen. Any grammar mistakes or sloppy writing remaining are my own fault, probably due to post-review writing she did not get to critique. I am grateful for her input that made the number of errors infinitely smaller than it otherwise might have been. I would also like to thank Eric Berglund, who spent untold hours editing my grammar and sentence structure, as well as deeply challenging my thinking. He forced me to craft many of my ideas with more precision and care, and this is a significantly better book because of his feedback. I am sure it is still not as good as Eric would like it to be, and for that I am truly sorry. Maybe we will get another chance to make it right.

I owe a debt of gratitude to the various members of The Clergy Project who were able to provide me with a safe, private, online support group. They allowed me to leverage their vast array of lessons learned so that my own coming out journey was far less painful than it might otherwise have been. Without them, this book would likely not exist.

Finally, I would like to thank R.E.M. for coming up with a haunting, thought-provoking, and memorable song from which the title of my book is taken. Wikipedia tells us that the phrase "Losing My Religion" has several possible meanings, including being at the end of one's rope. That's definitely what being at the end of faith felt like, but oh, what freedom I discovered in letting go and realizing that I could fly on my own!

1 GOING PUBLIC

"Does your religious belief require adherence without question, or does it seek to embrace truth, no matter to what conclusions that may lead? If you are convinced your religion is true, why fear inquiry? Why fear the discovery process, facts, and data?

Religion, it's time we had a talk. We had a good run, but it just isn't going to work out. I'm leaving you. It's not you, it's me. I have a compulsion to believe and practice what is verifiably true, and unfortunately, that's just not you. I'm sure you'll find a lot of others willing to swallow the blatant contradictions, circular logic, and the mental gymnastics they require, but I just can't do this anymore. I'm tired of pretending. I want something real, and I'm no longer afraid of the consequences of publicly seeking it out."

On January 6th, 2014 I posted the message above to Facebook. This was the first time I had publicly proclaimed my departure from faith. There were many public responses - attacks from believers who already knew about my deconversion, support from non-believers and tolerant Christian friends, and many statements of personal belief to counteract what I had just posted. This, however, was just the beginning of my coming-out journey - a stage set for the challenging discussion I was about to engage in.

On January 8th, 2014, I posted the following introduction to that discussion, which I would later use as a template for my future posts:

This is the first in what will be a series of posts detailing my deconversion journey. It is being put out there for anyone who wants to understand why I have walked away from my faith and is an open invitation for review and comment, but not snark or fight-picking. I *want* honest critique. I *want* to know if and where my thinking is off. Putting my ideas out there in public is absolutely intended to help me find the mistakes more so than to convert anyone to my line of thinking.

If you want to let me know you're reading but don't wish to comment, feel free to press the Like button. I will not be interpreting likes as statements of agreement with what I write for these.

As this is just an introduction, there are a lot of details that will come in later posts, so please respond only to what is in the doc and please wait to see what I actually write later about things mentioned but not explained. Thanks!

Apologies to those who have already seen this content in an earlier form during private or semi-private discussions. This is the first time I am making this public, so it will be new for many.

The link took readers to my official statement of coming out:

****

Why I No Longer Believe

I have been a believer for most of my life, involved in numerous leadership roles in a number of churches. I am a licensed Southern Baptist minister, and have been an avid defender of the faith for nearly two decades. I was the king of "complementary opposite" thinking and the concept of "progressive revelation" as a way to deal with the logical problems/ contradictions with some Old and New Testament teachings. Unfortunately for my faith in the supernatural, I deconverted as I continued to examine evidence. Things that I and other Christians engaged in science debates predicted we would find based on my (our) religious faith have proven incorrect over the course of the last decade or so. The naturalists, on the other hand, have been dead-on (and I will write more on those specific things over time). Honestly, then, for the past several years the only thing that had held me to my faith was the first cause[11] argument, but when I came across a reasonable alternative that required no more faith than the God hypothesis and lined up better with what we are discovering about our universe (again, I will come back to that topic soon), I was freed from my belief in anything supernatural.

Interestingly, the things that I feared would come to pass have not. I don't have less peace - I have more. I don't have more fear - I have less. Less certainty, sure, but more comfort in knowing that every movement of the universe is not some encrypted message that I must figure out in order to be in line with a God who will not speak clearly. Less anger and confusion about bad things happening to good people. Better alignment with what I know to be true and what I am allowed to believe. In fact, the only thing I fear now is the response from my religious family and friends - communities in which I am deeply embedded - but that is a risk I am finally willing to take.

I'm not militantly atheist. In fact, if I'm honest, part of me would love to believe in God again. My life would certainly be simpler, relationships, family conversations, activities, raising my kids, etc. As I was deconverting I prayed fervently for God to show me a way out. Letting go of my faith was terrifying. But, at the end of the day, any possible "proof" for God has a naturalistic explanation (trust me - I'm going to lay it all out there...), and in most cases, an easier one that lines up better with the facts as we know them today.

I'm still open on this subject, just like I've always been. God, if he's there, has an open invitation in my life, and I mean that with all my heart. If God exists, I really *do* want to know him! If he really cared for me like I used to believe (numbers the hairs on my head, knit me in my mother's womb and all), he would act upon my position, no? I can and would easily change my beliefs if the evidence - any evidence, really - shifted in that direction, but I'm not holding my breath on having a reason to do so. So my plan is to live my life as fully and abundantly as possible, without any pretense of the supernatural unless I have reason to believe, and then go to my final rest knowing I did the best I could with what I had in life.

---

[11] "Creation ex nihilo" - the apologetics argument that states everything in the universe is caused by something else, therefore for anything to exist, something outside the universe (supernatural) must have caused it.

****

What followed was an interesting mix of folks being thankful about being so open in my journey, looking forward to the conversations, and some who wanted to argue every point about why I was wrong at once. The main themes were:

> 1) Is it possible that this is just a deconstruction of your faith that you will later use to build a new one? Many people experience similar challenges to faith, but end up coming back to it.
>
> Answer: Sure. If new information becomes available that makes faith in the supernatural a reasonable belief, I will adjust accordingly. That said, this was by far not my first challenge to my faith. It was simply the first time that data had collected to the point where doubt made significantly more sense than belief. Then again, confirmation bias is a powerful thing, and I can be a slow learner at times.

> 2) What you should do is pray. Specifically, "Remove from me the things that keep me from You."
>
> Answer: Trust me - I was terrified of the unknown and the fear-based ramifications I thought this would have on my worldview. I prayed every version of that prayer I could think of. In the end, the facts did not change, and it turns out my fears were not only unjustified, but were 180 degrees in the wrong direction. I will write in detail about most of this in the days and weeks ahead, but for example: Letting go of belief in the supernatural didn't let me loose in a sea of amorality - it allowed me to be *more* moral than my bronze-age rules-based faith had. I thought I would fear death more, but once I had processed everything, I feared it *less* than I used to. Etc. At the time, I didn't believe that would be the case, so I prayed - a lot - "Lord I believe, please help me with my unbelief" and reached out to church leaders and other close friends of faith for prayer and support. I knew there would be a potentially heavy social and relationship toll to pay if I went down this road. Thus, this was not something I entered into lightly. In the end, reason and integrity won out over fear and pragmatism. But, that is also why I am now unrolling this in public. If I have erred or been sloppy in my journey, I'm trusting that someone in my sphere of influence will be able to point it out to me. That said, I have also been amazed at the number of folks I have come out to who

have replied something along the lines of "I'm in the same boat, but could never be honest with my friends and family about it." That is a terrible place to be in life, when you have to pretend you're something you're not. I hope my journey might help them as well, either to see my errors pointed out so they can also correct theirs, or maybe just to know that what they believe is legitimate and it's ok to be who they are (even if for them that still means keeping things quiet for whatever reason). Either way, this is a worthwhile adventure in my book.

Thus began my journey into laying out my personal beliefs for evaluation, critique, and debate. What would ensue in the coming days ended up being much larger than what I had originally planned, in part because people kept asking great questions that I thought deserved answers, and in part because I determined to keep nearly all of my individual posts focused and limited to about one-and-a-half 8.5" x 11" pages of typed text. There was a sense of accomplishment after this post, as I couldn't turn back at this point even if I had wanted. But I wouldn't have if I could. It was too exciting!

2 PASCAL'S WAGER

My post the morning of January 9th, 2014 started as follows:

> This is the second installment in my deconversion series of posts. In this one, I specifically address the oft-repeated "If I'm wrong, I've only lost a little time and money, so it's no big deal" mantra. It's one I often used myself as a believer, and it's an argument I am now convinced is flawed with potentially devastating ramifications on a societal scale.

From this point on, I ended each post with the same two paragraphs regarding why I was putting this out there, and how folks could let me know they were reading by pressing "Like" without fear of being interpreted as agreeing with me. This was always followed by the link to the latest installment.

****

My Problem with Pascal's Wager

Pascal's Wager is an argument that one should believe in God whether he actually exists or not. A wide number of variations on the theme have often been used by my Christian friends who I have come out to as a justification for their belief. Basically it says that the potential upside for believing in God, if God does exist, is enormous, whereas the potential downside if he does not is minimal over a short lifespan. Thus, the only rational thing to do is believe in God. Click here[12] for a more in-depth treatment on the topic.

There are many logical critiques of this idea that I don't really care for, even if I happen to agree with them. For example, what if your religion is

---

[12] http://en.wikipedia.org/wiki/Pascal's_Wager

worshipping the wrong god? There are a few thousand options to choose from, not just belief or nonbelief, so to be really safe, shouldn't you believe them all? But when folks would use that line on me, it turned out to be an exercise in mental gymnastics rather than an actual critique of faith. As a believer and apologist, if I could get the person to admit the possibility of gods, I could then logically show why the Christian God was the correct one. Thus, this one - while logically sound - rings hollow for me.

However, there is one significant problem in this line of thought that carries a lot of weight with me: It selfishly focuses only on the impacts of my actions on myself over my short lifespan (which are far greater than it gives credit for) and ignores the collective long-term societal effects of believing a lie, no matter how well-intentioned.

Believing a lie and proliferating it is not harmless. Sure, there is some good done by folks who believe they'll suffer eternal punishment if they don't, and even more good done by those who believe in a benevolent God who wants nothing more than for them to learn to love one another. The problem is that enormous resources are spent in activities that - if you are wrong - have no benefit to mankind whatsoever. Billions upon billions of dollars[13] that could be spent feeding the hungry or bringing water to children in lands that don't have it are spent on a "greater good" effort to spread the gospel. If, in fact, it is not true, then these billions of dollars and millions upon millions of well-intentioned man-hours are being completely wasted on something that isn't real. And that's the best-case scenario. On the darker end, you have the religious zealots who do things like blow up buildings and form militias to prepare for the boogey-man antichrist who is just around every corner, or neglect their families, or legislate against their gay neighbors, or convince the 10-year-old girl not to have an abortion and ruin her life because of some misconceived idea that the days-old tissue inside her has an eternal soul.

No, if you are wrong, there is an immense cost to you (time and money that could be spent on productive things) and to society for your misplaced belief, which wastes this tiny, precious sliver of life you are granted while on this planet. Seems like pretty high stakes to me.

****

---

[13] http://www.washingtonpost.com/blogs/wonkblog/wp/2013/08/22/you-give-religions-more-than-82-5-billion-a-year/

Responses to this post included several affirmations of the correctness of it - believing a lie, no matter how well intentioned, is never the best move for a society as a whole. Criticisms followed a predictable thread:

> 1) No thinking Christian claims Pascal's Wager as their primary reason for believing in God.
>
> Answer: - I agree with you wholeheartedly. For most folks it isn't their only argument, but when they're backed into a corner on the rest of what they believe, it's one that is often a fallback position as to why they don't need to worry about being wrong. I started here because I wanted to remove that as a logical retreat point [not that it stopped people from actually using it later on].

> 2) You appear to be able to talk yourself into believing anything.
>
> Answer: If that were true, I'd still be a believer. I W-A-N-T-E-D desperately to believe in God and Jesus. I was forced into nonbelief by honest evaluation, and as these posts continue, you will see why.

> 3) Without belief in God, we'd all be immoral hedonists. Why bother living purposefully if not for faith?
>
> Answer: I understand the fear, but categorically disagree. I promise to go into great depth on the morality issue in future posts.

> 4) You've obviously already decided what you believe. What's the point in discussing any of it?
>
> Answer: You're incorrect. I have determined what I now believe, and I have thought through this very carefully so will likely have considered most common rebuttals and objections, but it is wrong to conclude that is what I want to believe. If I just wanted to believe what I now believe, I wouldn't be doing what I'm doing. I'm making this effort in order to potentially change what I believe! You have to see that, right?

5) Isn't there value in most people believing in God even if he/it isn't real? Isn't religion responsible for many of the societal advances that we enjoy today?

Answer: To the historical value of religion, I am actually inclined to agree. I tend to fall in the "Patton Oswalt: Sky Cake" field of thought there. (Warning, strong and inappropriate language, but much more entertaining than reading my equivalent thoughts...)

https://www.youtube.com/watch?v=55h1FO8V_3w

6) God has left more than enough evidence to prove a foundation for anyone who WANTS to believe, but deliberately has provided enough ambiguity so that someone who doesn't want to believe still has the free will to make that decision.

Answer: If that is the case, I will be a believer at the end of this journey. If God doesn't exist, that's a convenient excuse for letting yourself off the intellectual hook.

7) What if your logic and science prove God doesn't exist, but in the end it turns out you're wrong?

Answer: I will address that in a future post. In short, I have nothing to fear if God is anything like you believe him/it to be.

And so, with that escape hatch closed, I continued to lay out the evaluation I had undertaken on my own faith. Believers were looking to take me out in one shot, and as a result asked lots of great questions. They would be disappointed to learn that I had - in every case - thought through the answers in great detail.

3 THE INERRANT BIBLE

I had successfully made my announcement to the world and had removed the safety hatch of Pascal's wager. There were three big challenges that had caused me to leave my fundamentalist Christian faith, and I wasn't sure which one to cover first: Biblical inerrancy, cosmology, and Biblical contradictions and immorality. I decided to come out swinging at Biblical inerrancy, since it is the cornerstone of what many people in fundamentalist Christian religions believe. On January 10th, 2014 I posted this:

> This is the third installment in my deconversion series of posts. There is no one single piece of information that led to my departure from faith, but rather a long string of data collected over time that finally pushed me over the line into nonbelief. This post covers what I think will be a big question mark for a lot of folks, a fact that is well known to nearly all seminary students but is almost never discussed outside of the classroom in conservative Christian circles or Sunday services.

****

Biblical Accuracy and the Virgin Birth

If you are a believer who claims that your holy writings are inspired and a source of truth, this by definition means the entire collection of writings must be incontrovertibly true. The unfortunate reality of this kind of a position is that if even one thing of significance can be proven incontrovertibly false or highly suspect, then the entire writing is now open to evaluation. In other words, for conservative Christians (like I was), the entire Bible must be true, and if a single part of it can be proven otherwise, their entire belief system can start to unravel.

For many, the biggest problems around this revolve around Old Testament challenges. In response, many Christians try to de-emphasize the Old Testament, a practice which I will address more fully in another post. In light of this, I prefer to start by examining the New Testament, and very specifically the canonical gospels. If the books that give us the story of Jesus contain a serious integrity problem or fundamental error, then the entire foundation is at risk, right?

What if the story of the virgin birth was the result of a clerical mistake, and it was a fulfillment of a prophecy that was never made?

First, a little back story. The "Bible" of the day for the writers of the gospels was the Greek Septuagint. Matthew 1:23 refers back to a verse in Isaiah 7:14, which is quoted as "The virgin will give birth to a son..." And, if one were to be using the Greek Septuagint of the day and were reading Isaiah 7:14, that is precisely what it claims. Unfortunately, this was a translation error.

Today, if you take nearly any New Testament class for Bible majors, when you cover this topic you will learn that the actual translation of Isaiah 7:14 does not refer to a virgin at all. It is a prophecy regarding a young woman of marrying age. Thus the virgin birth prophecy that Jesus supposedly fulfilled was one that was based on a translation error introduced centuries after it had first been written. It was not an actual prophecy Isaiah ever made, but the writer of Matthew (or most people of the time who used the Greek-language version of their scriptures) was probably unaware of this when creating and telling his account of Jesus.

"But wait!" you might say. "My Bible says 'virgin' in Isaiah 7:14!" And it is true that most English translations of the Bible do say virgin. Why? Because Matthew forces them into it. I still vividly remember Professor Gordon Dutille in my New Testament History for Majors class years ago recalling a conversation with a friend of his who was on the translation team for one of the English-language Bible projects. In short, Isaiah 7:14's meaning is very clear in the original language, but in the end, they chose to publish it as "virgin" instead of "young woman" in order - and I quote to the best of my memory here - "to avoid the political controversy that would ensue" if they chose to instead maintain their academic integrity.

Let's ignore for a moment the fact that even the most conservative estimates of when the gospels were written place them at 20-30 years after the death of Jesus. Let's ignore the failed prophecies of Jesus that believers have had to interpret as figurative or metaphysical even though they were clearly written to be literal. Let's ignore the fact that those who claim that the Old Testament isn't in force any more under grace are in direct conflict with Jesus himself in Matthew 5:17-19. Let's just focus on the fact that a key, celebrated, revered, and vigorously defended portion of the Jesus story was based on what we know today is a clear mistranslation of the original book of Isaiah and go from there. If you're willing to be intellectually honest with yourself, as a conservative Christian this is a serious problem.

If two of the gospels are on shaky ground even from their beginning passages, then they're not inerrant in any supernatural sense. It's really not too much of a stretch then to think that at least portions of them were fabricated stories rather than factual ones. This might have been done by well-meaning individuals recalling second-hand stories that grew as time passed. It could have been done by individuals who were writing specifically to make political or religious points for dubious reasons. I don't know the situation. What I do know is that I can't rely on them as sources of verifiable "God-breathed" truth. They just don't hold up to even the most basic scrutiny, if one is willing to really step back and scrutinize them.

That said, this is by far not the biggest problem with the Bible as a source of truth, in particular regarding how it describes and reflects the nature of God. More to come on that topic.

****

I knew this would be a shock for a lot of folks who had never taken a serious Bible or seminary class. The virgin birth is an article of faith for many, and for it to be based on a mistranslation? This one disturbed a lot of folks, for obvious reasons.

> 1) Sometimes some people get so smart or over study wrong literature that they forget their roots. Or as some might say " so smart they are stupid"

> Answer: That's exactly why I'm coming out in public. If something I've said is incorrect, illogical, or otherwise flawed, I WANT folks to point it out to me. However, simply stating I'm wrong doesn't meet any standard of conversation. You need to explain why.

2) Did you start hanging around or listening to the wrong people? Is that why you've left your faith?

Answer: No one is to blame for my departure from faith except for actually studying the Bible and keeping up with advances in science over the last decade. I performed my own research, and if you read my post, this particular chink in the armor was my New Testament History for Majors class.

3) If you've known this for 20 years, why are you just now acting on it?

Answer: This was a more than 20-year journey, and yes: I sat on this for 20 years and tried to integrate it with my faith. Eventually the weight of evidence became too great, and this was just one of the pieces that contributed.

4) Do you believe that Jesus was a historical figure? Regardless of whether he was the Son of God or a schizophrenic, do you believe he existed?

Answer: Honestly? I don't know. I think it's possible, but I haven't seen enough concrete evidence in either direction to come down conclusively on that. At the end of the day, even if he did exist, and even if some parts of the gospel accounts are based in fact, I don't believe there was anything supernatural about him, and from a faith perspective that's the part that matters most.

5) Aren't you afraid of going to Hell?

Answer: Not in the slightest, and later I will explain why I'm not worried even if I'm wrong.

6) You are wrong. People in that day had access to both the Greek and Hebrew texts, so they must have had a good reason for interpreting Isaiah like they did. Whether or not Jesus was born of a virgin was challenged early by skeptics, but the translation was not challenged, even by those who knew both languages.

Answer: There are many cultural reasons the Greek version of Isaiah might have chosen to interpret it as "virgin," including borrowing from other religious traditions at the time (for example, the Roman Dies Natalis Solis Invicti mythology). Also, in the time of Jesus, the Jews of Palestine no longer spoke Hebrew[14], therefore having access to the Hebrew versions of scripture wouldn't have automatically meant challenges to the accepted Greek translations.

However, let's assume you are correct - you now have another problem. This verse in Isaiah is understood to have been one of many Old Testament verses that was a dual-prophecy[15], and one that is understood to have been fulfilled in Old Testament times as well as to have a future meaning for the coming Messiah. You have one of two options then - either the Greek was a mistranslation (and Jesus was not born of a virgin), or the original Hebrew was fulfilled twice and there were two virgin births (which is clearly not being claimed.) Neither of these allow you to hold on to the inerrancy of scripture.

Again, this information was not new to me, nor is it a big secret among biblical scholars. I know the various ways Christians get around it, and I know the mental gymnastics required to do so. I also could have done a number of additional posts that would have further debunked Biblical inerrancy, however from a Christian fundamentalist perspective, a single error of this magnitude should be enough to crack the foundations of their entire belief system. This was enough - I had bigger problems with the Bible that I wanted to get to.

For more discussion on Isaiah 7:14:

http://en.wikipedia.org/wiki/Isaiah_7:14[16]

---

[14] Barker, Margaret (2001). "Isaiah". In Dunn, James D.G.; Rogerson, John. Eerdmans Commentary on the Bible. Eerdmans. (From Wikipedia link mentioned above)
[15] http://www.outreachjudaism.org/articles/dual-virgin.html
[16] I use many Wikipedia articles because they usually contain references and links to additional research that I might have otherwise used. Think of them as meta-references if you're uncomfortable trusting Wikipedia itself.

4 CREATION

January 11th, 2014 (morning):

This is the fourth installment in my deconversion series of posts. Why are we here? How can something come from nothing? These used to be serious challenges to a worldview without a supernatural explanation. Unfortunately for my faith, not any more.

****

<u>Science vs. Genesis 1:1</u>

For the longest time after I had lost my faith in the inerrancy of scripture (which I have already discussed once and will cover further later), the central thing that kept me hanging on to my Christian faith was the cosmological argument for the existence of the universe. Basically, modern versions of it go something like this:

* The universe is a static system with a set amount of matter and energy that have existed since the moment of its creation.
* Matter and energy cannot be created or destroyed, merely converted from one form to another.
* Therefore, in order for the universe to exist at all, some force outside of it must be the source of this initial infusion of matter from nothingness.

It was not much of a logical jump as a believer then to attribute to some "other-natural" or supernatural force the fact of existence. I knew of no good naturalist explanation (that didn't require as much or more faith than the God hypothesis) for why we were here until a few years ago when I learned about virtual particles[17] and quantum foam.[18]

It turns out scientists can actually observe empty space (with nothing in it) and watch particles randomly pop into and out of existence by some completely natural mechanism.[19] This means that the second part of the cosmological argument is wrong. As a result, I no longer need a supernatural explanation for the existence of matter and energy. Creating something from nothing, it turns out, happens all the time.

This induced a major shift in the necessity for the existence of the supernatural. If creation events happen all the time, then it's probable, and even likely, that a tiny fraction of these events are bigger than the ones we normally observe, and that in extremely rare cases you might have one big enough to cause something like our universe to happen. It is true that we have not actually observed this happening, but I hope we never do since being close enough to see it would probably destroy us. The fact that a completely natural mechanism exists that makes this a possibility is enough for me to say God isn't necessary to explain why we're here.[20] To be clear, one can still claim his existence, but you can no longer say that the origins of the universe are by necessity supernatural. Given all of the evidence against the Bible as inerrant and the full, twisted picture of the God it really painted (more to come), this was a powerful additional point in my deconversion, and the final piece of the puzzle that moved me into nonbelief.

****

---

[17] http://en.wikipedia.org/wiki/Virtual_particle

[18] http://en.wikipedia.org/wiki/Quantum_foam

[19] http://www.scientificamerican.com/article/are-virtual-particles-rea/

[20] Note: I do not claim with certainty that virtual particles are the mechanism for creation. There are additional theories being explored, many that may have merit. The fact that they exist at all, however, and thus could be the mechanism that sparked the universe was enough for me to drop the necessity for supernatural beliefs. If another, better natural mechanism is discovered in the future, that does not bother me in the slightest, nor does it make my discovery of virtual particles any less important as part of my journey away from belief in a supernatural God.

I found it interesting that Christians didn't respond to this post at all. They had previously challenged my lack of belief with the problem of existence, but largely had no rebuttals for this. One agnostic friend asked me about what would happen to my beliefs if I learned that virtual particles and quantum foam were proven to be false, but the science behind them is actually quite well established and the phenomenon consistently observed. I did have one Christian friend in a later post posit an alternative explanation that these particles might actually be traveling through time rather than popping in and out of existence, but that theory falls short because it doesn't explain why we always observe a matter / anti-matter pairing (since presumably that would be unnecessary for simple time-traveling particles.)

This was a critical piece of my deconversion story, and so it was one I was hoping for more of a fight on. Ironically, the most scathing attack on my idea came from another non-believer who claimed that there were better explanations for creation than virtual particles. I fully grant that the problem of creation is one that is not fully answered, and that several competing naturalist models exist that are being explored. The fact remains, however, that matter appearing from nothing happens without supernatural influence. Once you grasp that concept, determining the exact mechanisms that explain existence are relatively unimportant for this discussion.

5 FAITH

January 11th, 2014 (evening):

> This is the fifth installment in my deconversion series of posts. This post deals with an often-heard objection as I was coming out: "But you just have to have faith!"
>
> If you missed my fourth post on how science demonstrates creation events happening all the time, you should definitely check it out before reading this one. This will make a lot more sense if you do.

****

Faith and Deconversion

One of the more interesting revelations that has come from my coming out experience is the realization that almost no one who claims the mantle of Christianity actually believes that the Bible is really the inerrant word of God when pressed on the issue. Many who struggle to understand my departure from belief in the supernatural reject significant portions of the Bible for the same reasons I do. This astounds me. "What, then..." I will usually ask, "...is the basis for your continued belief?" And the answer so far has always been the same: Faith.

Faith is a word that can mean different things. I, even as an Humanist Bright[21], will wholeheartedly acknowledge that I have a tremendous amount of faith. For me, even as a believer, faith was always looking at the best available evidence and taking the next logical step based on that evidence. In my last post, I freely admitted that we have not actually observed a universe creation event, thus I cannot prove beyond doubt virtual particles are responsible. That said, it makes sense that they could be, and it lines up with the best available evidence, so I now believe that and will until better evidence comes along. That is by definition faith, and I very much have it.

For others, however, their faith means "belief without evidence" or worse, "belief despite evidence." They might reject the Bible as the inerrant word of God, but continue to believe in its Jesus figure - or at least the parts of the Jesus story they like. They create an ideal God - all loving, all good, all caring, etc. - by cherry-picking the parts of scripture that fit into their preferred view and simply ignore the rest of what the Bible says about him. Thus, it doesn't matter that the virgin birth is a fulfillment of a prophecy that was never actually made. It doesn't matter that God's commands usually seem to reflect the barbaric culture, rather than dictating that the culture reflect God's perfect love and goodness (more on that to come). In the end, you can reject all of the stuff in the Bible you don't like and just believe in a God of love (or hellfire and brimstone, whatever…) through "faith." Belief without evidence, or even despite evidence.

Let me try to put this worldview into perspective. Let's say I read in an ancient book that fairies are necessary in order for rainbows to exist, and I choose to believe it. I create a whole worldview in which there are billions of little supernatural creatures that have magic paintbrushes and fly through the sky after it rains painting water droplets and such. You, as a reasonable person, might rightly try to explain to me why those beliefs are silly. You might point out science around light, prisms, and water vapor and how rainbows are a natural and well-understood phenomenon. You might point out that the book that I got this belief from was steeped in ancient error, and no reasonable person would believe that fairies were necessary for rainbows to exist based on what we know today. And I might reply, then, that you simply have to have faith that it is true, and warn you that if you don't the fairies will give you pimples, warts, or worse.

---

[21] A Humanist is someone who believes in a lack of supernatural intervention in the universe. Humanists can either be Deists or atheists. A Bright is someone who does not believe in any supernatural existence. Thus, using both terms identified my life philosophy and my stance on the supernatural. http://www.the-brights.net/

You might laugh at this naiveté. However, if your definition of faith is "belief without evidence" or "belief despite evidence," what makes your beliefs any more credible than mine?

The answers here are amusing. "Well, because mine are true and yours are not!" The person has already admitted that there is no direct reason or evidence for their belief. On what basis, then, can they make that claim of truth? There is none, other than feelings and "personal experiences" which cannot be validated, tested, or even replicated (and I will dive deeply into personal experiences as a test for truth in a later post as well). Belief without evidence, and even belief despite evidence.

I believe most people to be reasonable, rational people, but I also believe most people to be blind to their own biases[22]. Most people will claim "faith" and "truth" around whatever they are taught as children. It is reinforced all throughout life and in the communities in which we/they live. Holy writings subtly (and overtly) warn us of the dangers of thinking about or testing your beliefs against reality and reason. "Don't think about or challenge the crazy parts of what you claim to believe to be true, or the evil one will get you." How convenient! Nearly ALL religions share these same types of warnings.

I reject faith defined as belief without or in spite of evidence, because to accept that means you have to accept all beliefs on equal grounds and just pick and choose right and wrong based on what you want to be true. There are objective ways to tell the difference between right and wrong, between truths and lies, and I propose that we should all be willing to examine all of our beliefs in light of the best available evidence. If that evidence points to the existence of the supernatural, then I will gladly follow it and become a believer with no regrets. If it doesn't, I refuse to even attempt to believe something that has no basis in truth. Given the available information, this seems to be the only way I can maintain my integrity.

****

This was the first post that I had to start deleting comments from some Christians for being just outright rude (For example: "I hope you and everyone who thinks like you like it hot, because that's how it's going to be in Hell.") This was also the first post that a family member - a cousin - elected to defriend me rather than continue to engage in the conversation.

---

[22] http://en.wikipedia.org/wiki/Confirmation_bias

But, as with the previous posts, there were no real critiques of the ideas, although a couple of interesting questions did come up. Most people wanted to shift the conversation to another topic I had not yet covered (evolution, thermodynamics, and morality, to name a few) and I had to keep reminding folks that I was just beginning the series and would cover all of those issues down the road.

> 1) I actually don't disagree with your "faith in spite of evidence" statement. I've had a good thing going for several decades now, so why change it? I've only got a few more decades to live, if I'm lucky. Who really cares what I believe? Society will progress with or without me.
>
> Answer: I will address this directly in a future post. If you're comfortable living a lie and aren't bothered by the evil that comes as a result, then stick with it. For me, there's too much at stake to do the same.

> 2) I'm really holding out for the Rapture. Nobody wants to see their parents get old and die. Everyone wants to think that their loved ones are in "a better place now". If you take away religion, aren't you also taking away hope and peace? Hope is a powerful thing.
>
> Answer: You are taking away a false hope and sense of security. In exchange, you gain an understanding of the true value of each life and an understanding of how important it is to make the world we live in better now rather than waiting for some nonexistent afterlife.

6 GOOD WITHOUT GOD

January 12th, 2014:

> This is the sixth installment in my deconversion series of posts. Ya'll just won't leave the issue of morality alone, no matter what else I post about, so here it is - the first post in a morality mini-series. How can there be good without God? Actually, it's inevitable. Natural human goodness is not only possible, it explains why we have survived as a species.
>
> If you've missed any of my previous posts in the series, I strongly recommend reading them before you get here. They tend to build on one another's ideas.

The second paragraph in this introduction, along with the other two I mentioned earlier, became a stock part of every post from here on out, as the ideas were now going to start building on each other in increasingly complex ways.

****

Morality Part 1: How Can There Be Good Without God?

Judging from the comments on my last few posts, many Christians (and probably those from other religions) find it difficult if not impossible to imagine how an atheist can have a basis for morality. Without an absolute standard for right and wrong - such as the supposed goodness of God (which I will address in much more detail in a later post) - why would humanity have developed morals and ethics at all?

It turns out the most likely answer is that on a societal level, behaving in ethical and moral ways bestows evolutionary advantage to societies that are genetically predisposed to behave in that manner. Thus, genes that make people naturally good have survived through natural selection. Let's make a few observations:

1) Humans are born with a natural propensity to be either selfish or selfless to varying degrees[23]. While we all have some capacity for selfishness and selflessness, we're all a little different in the degree and direction in which we would naturally go when left to our own devices.

2) Those natural propensities can either be reinforced or diminished by the overall culture of the society and environment in which a person lives.[24] Thus, a genetically selfless person can learn to become selfish in an overall selfish society, and a genetically selfish person can learn to become selfless in an overall selfless society.

3) Stronger, more efficient societies are more likely to be able to acquire resources and thus more likely to survive than weaker, less efficient ones.

Given these observations, picture a naturally selfish person engaging in a transaction of some sort. We would expect this person to maximize their personal gain in the transaction, even at the expense at the other person, and possibly up to and including cheating the other person in the transaction. This would appear to bestow on the selfish person an evolutionary advantage, since they appear likely to gain more than others might in similar transactions. The person on the other side of this transaction would learn the hard way about this person's selfish tendency and end up on the losing end of the deal.

Since better competition for resources = evolutionary advantage, the selfish person has the advantage - right? Not exactly. It is true that, in the short run, the selfish person wins, but over time the others in that culture will do one of two things: either adopt the tactics of the selfish person in order to try to gain advantage themselves, or alternatively become far less likely to deal with the selfish person at all. In either of these scenarios, the person's

---

[23] http://www.smithsonianmag.com/science-nature/are-babies-born-good-165443013/?all   and
http://en.wikipedia.org/wiki/Stanford_marshmallow_experiment
[24] Bickhard, Mark. How Does the Environment Affect the Person?
http://www.lehigh.edu/~mhb0/EnvtoPerson.pdf (Accessed 03/11/2014)

natural selfishness contributes to a cut-throat cultural environment which makes performing nearly any transaction extremely difficult and costly, if transactions can occur in that environment at all. Selfishness, it turns out, is great in the short term but costly in the long run, both for the person and for the overall society in which they live.

Economists call making decisions in light of what you expect the behavior of the other parties in the transaction a Nash Equilibrium. If you're interested in the research, this is a decent place to start:

http://en.wikipedia.org/wiki/Nash_equilibrium

Fortunately for morality (and humanity in general), Nash Equilibriums work in both directions. What happens in a society where the genetic predisposition is naturally selfless, and the general rule of how the members treat each other is the golden rule? Trust abounds, people are treated fairly, and transactions are easy and inexpensive. Sure, individuals are "leaving money on the table" with every individual transaction compared to a selfish person, but over the long run they are able to work together much more efficiently and produce a greater overall societal benefit. If we then follow our third observation and say that stronger (in this case, more efficient) societies are more likely to survive than weaker ones, we can then say that as decades and centuries pass, the more selfish the members of a society and the society as a whole are, the less likely they are to survive and thus pass on their naturally selfish genes. The opposite would be true for those naturally selfless individuals and societies.

None of this says that human beings are all naturally moral today, nor does it always mean that naturally, genetically moral individuals or even societies would always succeed as opposed to selfish ones. Indeed, the morality of a society is only one variable in a complex world where geography, access to natural resources, communication, and technology can all easily compensate for selfishness and allow "evil" societies to triumph over "good" ones over certain time periods. However, in the long run, selflessness in societies produces the benefits described above. All other things being equal, we will naturally become more and more selfless as a society or else lose out to one that is, both through genetic selection and the naturally reinforcing nature of selfless behavior over time. In the end, we are moral and tend to follow the golden rule as a species because it is in our overall long-term best interests to do so (you could say it's the ultimate form of selfishness), without any necessity for eternal rewards or anything supernatural in the equation. You don't need God to explain human goodness. Natural selection is all it takes.

More on the practical applications of this principle in my next post.

****

Some folks immediately recognized the themes in my paper and compared them to the work of evolutionary biologist[25] E.O. Wilson, and to a lesser extent, Kant's Categorical Imperative[26]. Other non-religious folks simply said "Well duh!" The most common mistake was to attempt to make this out to be some kind of definition of absolute morality, when in reality, I was only trying to provide an explanation for why moral behavior *as generally agreed upon by everyone* has survived via natural selection. Whether or not it was moral according to some external standard was beside the point completely. Other comments and questions:

> 1) There are really only two options: A) The universe was created by God. B) The evolutionary hypothesis - i.e. that all is the result of totally random chance. The evolutionary hypothesis is ridiculous. You and I work with complex systems every day. None of them "just happened". There is more chance of a tornado running through a junkyard and leaving behind a finished commercial airliner than there is for some of the simplest biological, chemical, and or physical processes to exist and work. Basic systems do not "evolve" into things that are more complex. There is no negative entropy in the universe.

> Answer: You are incorrect on three counts. Evolution is not totally random chance. It is primarily a result of organic response to changes in an environment via natural selection. I will write a primer on evolution to clear up this misunderstanding. Your second point is an argument from design (the tornado/airplane/junkyard hypothesis), which would be stronger if we didn't see so many problems in our designs that shouldn't be there if an intelligence was responsible for it. Your third misunderstanding is on entropy. In fact, there is negative entropy in the universe, all over the place, just not as a whole. I will write another post to address the arguments from design as well as the Second Law of Thermodynamics, which should help clear up these areas of confusion for you.

---

[25] http://en.wikipedia.org/wiki/Evolutionary_biology
[26] http://en.wikipedia.org/wiki/Categorical_imperative

2) People are innately wicked. You don't have to teach children to lie or be selfish and lazy. I, like the rest of humanity, would be nothing short of a barbarian if not for my belief in God. The genetic basis of goodness is just wishful thinking.

Answer: Nearly any research done in this area is going to hurt your supposition. For example, my two children are very different in terms of their natural sense of morality and ethics. We all possess the capability to do wrong, and if rewarded, are likely to repeat the behavior. However, it definitely comes more naturally for some and less for others (again, my kids are excellent examples of how wide the differences can be in different areas.) I also suspect that you are far from a barbarian, my friend, god or no god. You may choose to attribute your moral behavior to a supernatural force, but that actually just shows how truly moral you are - you don't want to even take credit for your own good behavior. You have good genes.

Keep in mind that my purpose for now is not to say that morality is absolutely the result of natural selection, but just to show that it could be. Once we've nailed that down well, I will then evaluate other possibilities, including the claim that morality comes from God, on its own merits and we will be in a place to compare the two proposals side by side. Nothing I have said so far has proven God couldn't be the source of morality or our universe. I've just shown that he's/it's not absolutely necessary as an explanation.

It would turn out to be a consistent problem in these discussions - folks either wanting to turn them into a discussion on absolute morality (which I eventually covered later in response) or folks claiming that they could still rationally believe that God was responsible for moral standards. As mentioned in my last comment above, my point wasn't to prove my theories correct, but rather that they were plausible. For intellectually honest folks, once you admit that the naturalist approach sounds plausible, it is only a matter of time before you have to start considering whether your continued belief in the supernatural is equivalent to believing fairies paint rainbows.

7 PERSONAL RELATIONSHIPS AND MARRIAGE

January 13th, 2014:

This is the seventh installment in my deconversion series of posts. If I no longer believe in the supernatural in any form, why am I not a hedonist? Am I free now to just do whatever feels good, as some have suggested in comments? In this post, I lay out a practical, personal, and very honest example of how the principles in my last post work in interpersonal relationships, and specifically my marriage.

****

Morality Part 2: Good Without God in Love and Marriage

In my last post I pointed out how Nash Equilibrium explains how genetic predispositions towards selfless behavior (following the "golden rule") led to evolutionary advantage for societies and their individual members. Is the same true with regards to individual relationships, and the most intimate one of them all - marriage? Now that I'm an atheist, does that mean I no longer need to worry about things like infidelity or treating my wife with love and respect?

Nope. Not even close. The genetic predisposition I possess to be faithful, loving, and respectful in my marriage actually provides me with significant personal benefits, and I would have to be an absolute fool to change the way I behave in any selfish manner for the potential gain available.

Marriages are transactions. No two are exactly alike, but in general two people in marriages are trading resources for personal (and mutual) benefit. Sexual satisfaction, financial resources, companionship and entertainment, safety and protection, and workload-sharing are just a few of the potential "goods" that are exchanged.

Let's pick one of these areas and put it in context with our selfish / selfless example. In a traditional marriage (like mine) the understood agreement is for some of these exchanges to be exclusive between the two partners, and specifically and perhaps most strongly the sexual relationship part. When my wife and I were married, we made an agreement to keep sexual activity exclusively between the two of us. If either of us were to engage in sexual behavior with another person - including flirting and other behaviors that don't involve physical contact but were bent in that direction - we would be in violation of our agreement. But, let's face it - my wife and I are both human beings and sexual creatures (with apologies to my children for the unavoidable imagery when they read this…) Both of us are wired to want to have sex with other attractive people, and would probably find those extra-marital experiences sexually satisfying. Why, then, don't we engage in them?

In a marriage relationship, you agree on ground rules, and you get lots of opportunities to test each other in their application. In my marriage, I know that in the short run sexual adventures with other people would be potentially fun and pleasurable, but in the long run I would lose my wife's trust, and in the process lose a lot of the value in my marriage. It might end completely, or transition into a relationship where we were continually harming each other in an attempt to not be the one hurt the most by the other one. Frankly, I can't imagine any amount of sexual pleasure being worth risking the kind of relationship and trust my wife and I have built over the past two decades.

Is there a scientific, naturalist explanation for this morality? Indeed there is: an application of the Nash Equilibrium known as The Prisoner's Dilemma[27] . This scenario describes a situation where two criminals have been captured and are being interrogated. If one of them confesses and testifies against their partner while their partner remains silent, they will get to go free while their partner will spend three years in prison. If both of them confess fully to each other's crimes, they both will serve two-year sentences. If neither confesses, they will serve shorter sentences of only one year. The

---

[27] Toby Ord and Alan Blair, 'Exploitation and peacekeeping: introducing more sophisticated interactions to the iterated prisoner's dilemma'. http://amirrorclear.net/academic/papers/sipd.pdf

criminals are then taken to separate rooms and given the opportunity to confess. What happens?

If the prisoners have a history, trust each other, and want to work together in the future, odds are neither of them will confess. They both lose a little, but avoid the risk of long prison terms and protect the relationship in the process. If they do not trust each other, then they both will confess rather than risk being betrayed and getting the longest possible sentence for themselves. Just as in our selfish vs. selfless society discussion, trust = better overall outcomes for everyone involved.

It is easy for me to give up the short-term sexual gain an affair might bring in exchange for the deep, lasting relationship I have with my wife today, and I have complete faith that she feels the same way. No longer believing in God has not changed that one bit on my part, and the field of economics once again provides a strong framework for explaining why this is true.

For more on The Prisoner's Dilemma, start here:

http://en.wikipedia.org/wiki/Prisoner's_dilemma

****

Many folks supported these arguments by providing statistics - for example, atheists are very underrepresented in prison populations compared to their percentage of the general population, lower divorce rates than believers, etc. The fact that I centered this post on my marriage garnered some interesting responses, all generally around the same theme.

> 1) If there is no God, there is no sin, so what is the purpose in making promises to someone officially (marriage) to keep commandments from the one who gave life to them, if there is ultimately no account for our life here on earth when we die?
>
> Answer: The point of the post is not to prove that God isn't responsible for morality (and in this case, marriage fidelity), but to show how we can explain morality without him. Once that is established, in future posts I intend to fully explore what God says about marriage in the Bible (as well as other moral issues), and hold that up in comparison to my stated positions. At that point, everyone will have the ability to judge for themselves which of the two more likely explains their own moral behavior, as well as any moral behavior exhibited throughout humanity.

2) I know people that have open marriages and they think they have good marriages. And if their idea of marriage is good, then they would have no problem having sex with someone who is partnered in "marriage" with someone else because it is not wrong to them. So, how is anything, then, really good?

Answer: What I did was to apply a natural moral principle (the Prisoner's Dilemma) and show that it explained the fidelity in my marriage without necessity for supernatural laws. It also explains why I'm generally nice to people in one-on-one relationships of any kind and do not go around just doing whatever I want to whomever I want, regardless of what I think I could get away with. You are correct, though, in that this does not necessarily prove that having multiple sexual partners when married is innately wrong. Then again, neither does the Bible, which seems to be on board with polygamy all over the place. In fact, it's practically a command in Deuteronomy 25:5-6. (Note it does not stipulate a different action if the brother already has a wife...)

3) Someone else may feel you are oppressing your wife (and yourself) of free sexual expression with your "morals" and would have the obligation then to make sure your wife has the opportunity to express herself in spite of you. That is not wrong. After all...it feels good.

Answer: You miss the point of my marriage example completely. Yes, it would feel good to have sex with other people, but that feeling must be considered in light of the cost, in which my wife (in your scenario) would need to consider the overall value of our marriage to her if I engaged in the same behavior. Over time, we end up moving from being the 1-year prisoners to the 2-year prisoners (in the prisoner's dilemma example) in exchange for very temporary rewards. It isn't oppression - there's nothing I can physically do to stop my wife from having an affair - but rather a cost-benefit analysis of the various options and making choices that end up producing the highest personal reward. I'm faithful because I'm selfish, in the long run.

Consider this: If I were truly selfless, I would want my wife to experience pleasure at every opportunity, without regard for my own feelings and needs, and vice versa. Sorry, but that's not me. That said, if that is you, I have no moral opposition to that stance. :)

8 MORAL AMBIGUITY

January 14th, 2014:

> This is the eighth installment in my deconversion series of posts. We have explained how human morality is inevitable on a societal scale and on a personal relationship level due to long-term effects of repeated transactions. What about morality in terms of activities that don't involve or affect other people? Is there a natural mechanism available to outline individual morality as well? Put another way, do atheists have a basis for teaching behavioral ethics to their children in situations when the primary person involved is just themselves?

****

Morality Part 3: Good Without God, Moral Ambiguity, and My Kids

In my previous two posts I have detailed Nash Equilibriums and The Prisoner's Dilemma, and how in the long run selfless behavior provides an evolutionary benefit and is thus genetically imprinted and naturally selected. Now that we've laid this groundwork, we can boil all of this down into an extension of the golden rule that I like to refer to as the "Platinum Rule." I find it easy to remember as a little couplet:

"Do unto others as you would have them do
  if you were that person and they were you."

This simple phrase does a really good job of codifying what we have discussed so far with regards to how we should treat one another. (We have already thoroughly discussed why.) The original golden rule could be twisted to say "Well, if I were gay, I'd want someone to scare it out of me so I could avoid Hell" as a justification for angry or violent behaviors towards homosexuals. The Platinum Rule makes that justification harder because you have to see the world through their eyes, not from your own perspective.

That said, there are aspects to morality that are not obviously covered by this principle - specifically, moral decisions that are based on actions you take and activities you participate in that primarily affect you rather than another person. Rules-based systems (i.e. "do what the Bible says") simplify the decision-making process in these situations in the same way Santa Claus can affect a small child's decision to throw a tantrum or not on December 23rd. Right and wrong are clearly defined, as are punishments and rewards (be they real or imagined.) Unfortunately, as I will write about later, these rules are not always vetted via the Platinum Rule, and as such can contain significant moral errors. As teenagers and adults, we need the ability to think through issues in a more sophisticated way.

With my kids, I have always handled these issues based on expected outcomes rather than rules, even as a believer. When discussing topics like pre-marital sex with my now teenage daughter, I would frame discussions around questions like "...and why do you think the Bible says what it says?" rather than commanding "Don't do it because the Bible says so." This led to lots of productive discussion around how relationships form, how good and bad relationship habits develop, some honest sharing about regrets from some of my teenage relationships, and **allowing my daughter to build her own set of sexual mores based on the concept of short-term gain vs. potential long-term consequences, all without the need for supernatural influence.**

Practically speaking, whenever we discuss issues that are not easily answered by simple observation of the Platinum Rule - alcohol, drugs, lying, cheating, work ethic, etc. - I usually ask "What does the 25-year-old version of yourself hope you do about it?" She is usually able to answer her own question - often with a sigh. :) If she's not sure, then we get to have an in-depth discussion on the subject and discuss pros and cons until she is.

In case you missed what I did there: I have created a construct by which decisions about behaviors that affect only her are actually transactions being made with another person - the future version of herself. This allows the application of the Platinum Rule for greatest personal effect.

I'm not saying that her decisions are necessarily always better than anyone else's, but she makes them based on logic, forethought, and the consideration of long-term consequences rather than some arbitrary set of rules cherry-picked from bronze-age documentation claiming to be of supernatural origin.

Full disclosure: With my kids, I stack the deck in my favor at every opportunity. My daughter goes to a private Christian school. Our motivation for this decision includes the teaching of behavioral morals, which doesn't happen to the same extent in public schools as it does in hers. I think this focus has a lot of value even if I no longer agree with every single one of their moral foundations. I personally believe that a lot of religious morality has survived over the centuries because it knowingly or unknowingly encouraged the kind of behaviors that lead to better long-term outcomes (see Morality Part 1 for an in-depth discussion on this.)

It is this kind of thinking that I want to use to evaluate my own decisions, and also pass on to my kids: moral behavior means treating others like you would want to be treated if you were them and they were you + making decisions that the you in the future will be happy with, which usually means short-term sacrifice for long-term gain. You usually get to the right place by following these principles, no supernatural forces required.

****

Not many responded to this one, other than to say they admired the way I applied the Platinum Rule to child-rearing and made what are typically considered moral decisions into transactions with a future self. I did get some good questions on the overall moral picture I was painting, however.

> 1) I will admit that your thinking is internally consistent. The views you are espousing (all relationships are transactions, etc.) is true to a point, and consistent with well-known behaviorist / materialist viewpoints. For me, this seems to be a profoundly reductionist way of characterizing how we think about human relationships.
>
> If everything in our lives is a question of "What's in it for me?", on what basis does anyone get to impose the "Platinum Rule" or any other ostensibly beneficial standard on those who may not believe the same things about the importance of being 'nice' that you do?
>
> Answer: As I've said before, my purpose in the three morality posts so far has not been to prove that these theories are true, but rather that they're plausible (and if not, find out why not.) Your admission that

my thinking is at least internally consistent was exactly the kind of feedback I'm looking for - not that you agree, but you can see how I got there. Thank you.

I'm also not trying to argue that the Platinum Rule is "objectively" true - only that it is useful in producing the best possible outcomes for human society in general (due to Nash Equilibrium, etc.) and as such, should be followed consciously for the best results. It's learning by observation, not by diktat.

2) I've known you for many years. The fundamentalist Christian worldview which you argue against is not one to which you fully ascribed as a Christian – yet the standard of 'proof' you demanded (and were ultimately unable to meet) always seemed to me to be a vestigial remnant of your early spiritual and intellectual formation in that tradition.

Answer: This is primarily for the many, many fundamentalist friends I have made over the past 30+ years who would simply dismiss any claims I make by stating that the Bible is the ultimate source of truth, given its inerrant status. If you already buy into the concept that the Bible is fallible, then there's nothing to debate on that point. I'm also trying to be very careful and only make one point at a time - i.e. I have not yet produced any actionable conclusions given that the Bible is fallible, other than the fact that the Bible is fallible and thus what it says must be examined for accuracy just like anything else.

3) Regardless of which side of this whole argument one comes down on, there is no 'proof' (your rhetoric sometimes sounds as though there is) – only a preponderance of EVIDENCE which leads one to a certain set of conclusions.

Answer: BINGO! You've hit on probably the most important topic of all. The question is not which worldview can be definitively proven (exactly as I stated in my Faith article) since evidence is likely always going to be incomplete. The question is in which direction does the best evidence point? Given what we know, what is most likely to be true? So far I have approached morality, for example, from the standpoint of "is there a reasonable explanation to explain its existence other than God?" The next part of the question is "Is the God of the Bible actually moral?" Once we've evaluated those two concepts, you are free to judge for yourself which of the two views does a better job explaining your own morality, much less any morality we see in the world today. All I intend to do is lay out evidence, and specifically some of the evidence that moved me from belief to nonbelief.

I found this last exchange to be particularly honest and refreshing. My efforts towards building a case for naturalist morality were being acknowledged, even if not agreed with. It was difficult for me to limit my posts to one per day. I was interested in seeing how Christians were going to respond to the morality portrayed in the holy book they claimed as its source.

9 EVOLUTION

January 15th, 2014 (morning):

This is the ninth installment in my deconversion series of posts. Is natural selection / evolution really just a convenient out for someone who doesn't want to believe in God? I'm going to hit pause on the morality mini-series and do a two-fer today on some topics that have been floating around in the comments and in private conversations. This first one is an attempt to clear up what I think is clearly a misunderstanding that some people have about the way natural selection works to cause evolution. Later today I will post about a couple of related apologetic arguments (Arguments from Design and the Second Law of Thermodynamics) and break down why they fail as proofs for existence of the supernatural. Please make sure that you discuss the correct topics in the correct thread! We'll get back to the morality mini-series tomorrow.

****

Primer on Evolution via Natural Selection

Given some comments that have been made regarding evolution, it is clear to me that there is a great deal of confusion regarding what natural selection is and how it works.

Let's start by clearing up a common misconception: evolution by natural selection is not a random process[28]. It is a process by which species evolve

---

[28] http://evolution.berkeley.edu/evolibrary/article/evo_32

based on the conditions of their environment. It happens all the time, and in non-controversial ways.

For example, say there are butterflies whose population contains those that have natural camouflage in their environments. They are harder to see, and thus they are more likely to survive than most of their brightly-colored cousins. However, of those brightly-colored ones, some of them are naturally faster than others, and this speed also serves as a way to escape predators. Over time, slow and brightly colored butterflies are more likely to get eaten and thus unable to pass on their genes. As time passes, the butterflies that are left will mate and produce offspring, which will contain random distributions of the fast brightly-colored and slow camouflaged genes. Some of those offspring will end up slow (from the camouflaged parents) and brightly colored (from the other parent) and will have a greater chance of being eaten, thus unable to pass on those genes. Some will be born camouflaged and slow, some bright-colored and fast, and some very lucky ones will be born both camouflaged and fast. Those in the last group are the most likely to survive of all, and as predators evolve in response to their easy food supply dwindling, eventually they're almost all that is left.[29]

Almost no one disputes this kind of "micro-evolution" as it is sometimes referred to. It's non-controversial in many respects because the butterflies are still clearly butterflies - they're just colored differently and can fly faster. What is specifically rejected by some biblical literalists are the concepts of evolution of complex life from simple organisms, and equally as vehemently, the fact that humankind and other primates evolved from a common ancestor. Since the principles are identical between the two, we'll cover what I believe to be the more interesting one: man's relationship to other primates.

Let's quickly clear up another common misconception: evolution does not say that man evolved from chimpanzees or our even closer relatives, bonobos. What it says is that at some time in our history (estimated to be about six million years ago), we shared a common ancestor. There are a number of reasons to believe this is true. In the last decade we have

---

[29] This example was pulled from an ingenuous interactive exhibit at the Saint Louis Science Center in which the viewer was the predator and touching the screen to get the most butterflies possible in a certain time limit. Inevitably, slower and brightly colored butterflies were caught first. When the remaining butterflies were then genetically recombined, the population remaining became harder and harder to catch as it became faster and more camouflaged over successive generations.

uncovered fossil evidence of early humans with specifically chimp-like features, smaller brains, etc. In addition, our relatively new ability to read genetic code has demonstrated that we are nearly 99%[30] genetically identical to our primate cousins. That sounds close, and it is, but when you consider our genetic code is made up of billions of characters, a 1.3% difference actually means millions of coding differences. (For reference, humans differ in their genetic code by a range of about 0.1%[31].) That said, six million years is a long time for those changes to have taken place.

The question then is why those differences exist in the first place, and why don't we see creatures that are 99.4% human - sometimes referred to as a "missing link"? The answer is actually fairly simple though, and involves the same processes as the butterfly example above.

When speciation first took place around six million years ago, the branch that led to chimps and bonobos existed in an environment where raw strength and agility in tree-climbing environments provided greater opportunity for survival. Thus, those members of our ancestor species that had traits that lent themselves to those environments were more likely to survive (just like the camouflaged and fast butterflies), whereas those born with larger brains and ability to run great distances over longer time periods but without that kind of agility and strength were less likely to survive in that environment. On the other side of the family tree, members of our ancestor species that eventually became humans found themselves in environments where intelligence and ability to run long distances led to greater chance of survival. Those born with extra strength and climbing agility but with smaller brains and less mobility on land were less likely to survive in that environment.

Of course there are many more than just those four variables at play in survival, but hopefully simplifying it down to just those helps make the discussion clear. Over millions of years, for the human side of the branch, those who were born smarter and better runners were better and better able to survive, and became the equivalent of the fast camouflaged butterflies in their environment. The same thing happened on the chimpanzee/bonobo side of things, but their equivalent of fast and camouflaged was strength and climbing agility. Slowly, ever so slowly, the different branches grew further and further apart - each one adapting to its own environment in the most efficient manner based on who was least likely to get eaten where they

---

[30] Depending on how you evaluate the genome, the actual percentage is between 96% and 99%.
[31] http://en.wikipedia.org/wiki/Human_genetic_variation

were - and became what we see today as modern chimpanzees/bonobos and modern humans. As to no missing link, there simply wasn't an environment in which a different combination was able to survive better than those two, which is why we don't see those creatures running around today.

One final side-note: If this is true, then it should be theoretically possible for us to modify genetic code and produce hybrid creatures - either undo or modify the effects of natural selection. While there are many significant ethical issues involved in doing this kind of work with humans and chimps, scientists have actually shown that this is possible in other animals. If you haven't seen it before, this will probably blow your mind:

http://www.dailymail.co.uk/sciencetech/article-2027558/Scientists-undo-evolution-create-chicken-maniraptora-snout.html

For more on the human genome, here's a great starting point:

http://en.wikipedia.org/wiki/Human_genome

****

Perhaps unsurprisingly, despite a great deal of energy put into the conversation around how the idea of evolution was ridiculous, no one commented on where this post fell short. The earlier arguments had revolved around incorrect assumptions about evolution via natural selection, which I had addressed in this post, as well as topics such as negative entropy (the problem of moving from less to more complexity) and apparent design. I would cover those in a separate post later that day. One supporter recommended Jerry Coyne's very good book: *Why Evolution is True*[32]. I second that recommendation.

---

[32] http://www.amazon.com/Why-Evolution-True-Jerry-Coyne-ebook/dp/B001QEQRJW

10 FAILED APOLOGETIC ARGUMENTS

January 15th, 2014 (afternoon):

> This is the 10th installment in my deconversion series of posts, the second for today. In this one I'm going to address a couple of apologetic arguments used to discredit evolution - the Second Law of Thermodynamics and Arguments from Design - and explain why they fail as proofs for existence of the supernatural. We'll get back to the morality mini-series tomorrow.

****

Failed Apologetic Arguments: Entropy and Design

In a recent conversation, a good friend of mine brought up some great apologetic arguments. As a well-researched apologist myself for nearly 20 years, I had not only heard (and used) them all before, but had to come up with answers to them as part of my journey.

Entropy and the Second Law of Thermodynamics

Entropy can be thought of as disorder which, oddly enough, leads to an eventual end-state of equilibrium. The Second Law of Thermodynamics[33] states that entropy always increases. On a universal scale this law states that on average all things move from more complex to less complex - for example, stars eventually expend their fuel into heat that eventually dissipates equally across the universe. In other words, the universe is winding down.

---

[33] http://hyperphysics.phy-astr.gsu.edu/hbase/thermo/seclaw.html

No one argues that the law is incorrect; however creationists (including myself back when that label applied to me) have tried to use it as a reason why evolution goes against science and reason. If everything is moving from more to less complex, how could life have evolved from simple chemicals to hairless primates typing Google docs?

The key here lies in the parameters around entropy. It always increases *on average* on a universal scale. However, if you evaluate a system inside the universe to which energy is constantly being added, that energy can move things in the other direction.

Our planet is not a closed system. Our sun is constantly bombarding it with large amounts of energy which are converted in a number of ways to create the conditions that allowed for and sustain life as we know it, and this has been going on for billions of years. Thus, while average entropy is increasing on a universal scale, entropy on our planet with regards to life can easily be explained as having decreased via natural means because of this outside energy being added to the system. This does not violate the Second Law of Thermodynamics in any way.[34]

Arguments from Design

One common argument creationists use in discussions is the "airplane in a junkyard" illustration. Basically it states that life on our planet is so complex and the conditions for it to exist so unlikely that it would be easier to believe a tornado blew through a junkyard and as a result assembled a perfect Boeing 747 completely by chance.

There are two problems with this argument. The first one is that it assumes that life on our planet is so well constructed that there can be no question regarding an intelligence behind it. If, on the other hand, the designs we see in life contain significant and unnecessary flaws, then the airplane in a junkyard analogy falls apart (pun intended). The second problem relates to how improbable life actually is. Say the odds of life developing by natural selection are one in 10 billion, but there are hundreds of quadrillions of environments in which life might possibly be able to develop. It then becomes nearly mathematically impossible for life to not develop purely by chance, if that's the case.

---

[34] http://en.wikipedia.org/wiki/Entropy_and_life

The first problem is easy to evaluate. Life is full of examples of bad design. Humans consume food in the same orifice used for breathing. An intelligent designer would have avoided this high risk of death by choking by separating those two systems. Other human examples include the existence of the appendix, largely useless nerves and muscles, common malformation of the human spinal column, and various problems avoided or advantages enjoyed by other animals compared to humanity.

For more on this, check out this link:
http://en.wikipedia.org/wiki/Argument_from_poor_design

To the improbability vs. number of chances for occurrence, first we start with an assessment: How many stars exist which can potentially provide energy needed to overcome entropy and produce life on one of its planets? It turns out in the "observable" universe, there are approximately 170 billion galaxies. If we assume that each galaxy had the same number of stars as our Milky Way galaxy, there are roughly 10^{24}, or one septillion stars.

http://www.universetoday.com/102630/how-many-stars-are-there-in-the-universe/

For an evaluation of what that means regarding the possibility of life, I'll refer you to this work:

http://infidels.org/library/modern/richard_carrier/addendaB.html

The main thing I'll point out is a reminder that there is a significant difference between "random chance" and "natural selection." Natural selection is an unguided process (i.e. no supernatural influence) but is far from random. In short, given the number of stars and thus possibilities for life, it is really inevitable that life was going to emerge in our universe via natural selection, and we're just some of the lucky ones that get to benefit from that occurrence.

****

Like the post before, there were no comments in response to this post. I began to worry I was losing everyone's interest. That turned out to be a false fear!

11 CHILD SACRIFICE AND GOD

January 16th, 2014 (morning):

> This is the 11th installment in my deconversion series of posts. Often I am asked who or what is responsible for my deconversion, and the response is not one people generally expect: "The Bible." In my experience, people tend to cherry-pick scriptures to obey, and ignore the stories or commands that don't line up with their sense of right and wrong - yet somehow will still claim that the Biblical God is their source of truth. In the next few installments in the morality series, we will take a look at some of the more shocking and almost never discussed examples of clear immorality in scripture, and ask the very, very difficult question: Does the morality in scripture paint a picture of a being worth serving, even if it does exist?

****

Morality Part 4: Child Sacrifice in the Name of God

In discussions on morality, people often claim that without God (and Jesus) there is no basis for morality. I have fully addressed the fact that morality has a potential basis in nothing more than natural selection, however until now I have not made the case that this basis is more likely or more accurate than the God hypothesis. In this post we will go on a journey through scripture - often scripture passages that are rarely, if ever, talked about in church settings - and see if the morality of God as depicted in the Bible is consistent and good by any standard.

I realize this topic is tough for some people. For some of you, even questioning whether the God of the Bible is moral or not is like an ant questioning human behavior. If you fall into this category, then feel free to reframe this - not as a question of whether God is good, but whether your concept of God and his morality is accurate. All I am going to do is use scripture, and for the most part let the Bible speak for itself.

Some people will try to minimize the examples below because they are from the Old Testament. Just keep in mind to do this puts you at odds with Jesus in Matthew 5:17-19. If you believe Jesus was God and perfect, and believe this passage to be true, you have to integrate Old Testament morality with your concept of God's perfect morality. In addition, Hebrews 13:8 states that Jesus - as God - is the same throughout all eternity. Thus, the God who commanded adulterers be stoned was the same God who forgave the adulterer in John 8:1-11. Neither the Bible nor Jesus give you any option to come to a different conclusion. If scripture is true then God and Jesus are one, God is the same throughout eternity, and the ministry of Jesus did exactly as he said, and thus did not nullify the Old Testament law in the slightest sense - at least not from a moral standpoint. It is upon this standard that I will base my examination of God's morality.

The Child That Was Sacrificed
in Exchange for Victory on the Battlefield

Normally when we hear about human sacrifice, we talk about Abraham and Isaac. We like that story because in the end, God stops Abraham from sacrificing the boy and instead provides a ram in the brush as a replacement. However, in a seldom-discussed other story of scripture, a man offers to sacrifice to God the first thing that comes out of his house if God will grant him victory on the battlefield. He is indeed successful, and upon returning home, the first thing to come out of the man's home is his daughter, an only child. What do you think happens next?

****

Judges 11:29-40   New International Version (NIV)

Then the Spirit of the Lord came on Jephthah. He crossed Gilead and Manasseh, passed through Mizpah of Gilead, and from there he advanced against the Ammonites. And Jephthah made a vow to the Lord: "If you give the Ammonites into my hands, whatever comes out of the door of my house to meet me when I return in triumph from the Ammonites will be the Lord's, and I will sacrifice it as a burnt offering."

44

Then Jephthah went over to fight the Ammonites, and the Lord gave them into his hands. He devastated twenty towns from Aroer to the vicinity of Minnith, as far as Abel Keramim. Thus Israel subdued Ammon.

When Jephthah returned to his home in Mizpah, who should come out to meet him but his daughter, dancing to the sound of timbrels! She was an only child. Except for her he had neither son nor daughter. When he saw her, he tore his clothes and cried, "Oh no, my daughter! You have brought me down and I am devastated. I have made a vow to the Lord that I cannot break."

"My father," she replied, "you have given your word to the Lord. Do to me just as you promised, now that the Lord has avenged you of your enemies, the Ammonites. But grant me this one request," she said. "Give me two months to roam the hills and weep with my friends, because I will never marry."

"You may go," he said. And he let her go for two months. She and her friends went into the hills and wept because she would never marry. After the two months, she returned to her father, and he did to her as he had vowed. And she was a virgin.

From this comes the Israelite tradition that each year the young women of Israel go out for four days to commemorate the daughter of Jephthah the Gileadite.

****

If God is truly in control of all things, he could have caused the family pet to walk out of the house before the daughter. He could have sent an angel to intervene like he did in the Abraham/Isaac story[35]. He could have stopped this tragedy performed in his name by his champion by any number of means, but he did nothing. Is this the God you thought you served?

Some will try to justify God's lack of action by stating that he did not specifically command that this child be sacrificed and will thus imply that he did not approve. Unfortunately, you cannot get that interpretation from a clean reading of the story, and instead must try to impose some supposed nature of God that remains completely silent in the text. It's just not

---

[35] http://en.wikipedia.org/wiki/Binding_of_Isaac

intellectually honest, as one could do the same to imply evil intentions when God is supposedly portrayed as good in other passages. No, the message is clear: this child was sacrificed to God in exchange for victory on the battlefield, and he did nothing to stop it from happening.

In the next post, we'll look at what God says regarding rape and human dignity.

****

The discussion here was very interesting to me. Many folks had not heard of this story and were not aware of a recorded successful child sacrifice in the name of God. To be clear, Christians have ways of engaging in what I call "mental gymnastics" and can find ways around this story while still giving God a pass, and by itself, I openly admit that this story does not prove God immoral. One of my friends wrote a multi-page response along those lines. That said, as part of a larger picture - which I was getting ready to paint - it shows us an image of God that does not line up with the "all knowing, all powerful, all-loving" God that Christians claim him to be.

I also received a very interesting comment from a Catholic friend, who let me know that in his tradition, they viewed the Old Testament as "God inspired" but basically stories set to teach lessons. In this case, the lesson was don't make promises to God lightly. Thus, inerrancy is not nearly as significant in a tradition like that as it is in the one in which I grew up and lived.

My positioning had always been that the Bible was true. If so, I then had to integrate these (and many, many other) items that I would be discussing with my picture of a loving, just, moral God. If you are already convinced that the Bible contained errors, then the next few posts on morality really don't apply to you, and should just be considered interesting side discussions.

12 GOD ON RAPE AND HUMAN DIGNITY

January 16th, 2014 (afternoon):

> This is the 12th installment in my deconversion series of posts, the second one for today. In continuing to examine the morality of the Bible, I will now turn to a delicate couple of issues for a lot of folks: rape and human dignity. Please consider this a trigger alert for my friends to whom that applies. I hate to have to dive into such terrible areas, but looking eyes-wide-open into what scripture actually said on these topics was a difficult but necessary part of my deconversion process. Please use discretion, and commenters, please be extra sensitive in what you say in response. Thanks guys.

****

Morality Part 5: God on Rape and Human Dignity

In the previous post I discussed the standard the Bible forces us to use when judging God's morality: God and Jesus are one, God is the same throughout eternity, and the ministry of Jesus did exactly as he said in Matthew 5, and thus did not nullify the Old Testament law in the slightest sense - at least not from a moral standpoint. Using this lens, we will now examine several laws that pertain to rape, slavery, and human dignity.

Rape

Deuteronomy 22 has an amazing array of God's commands when it comes to dealing with rape victims and aggressors, starting with verse 23. If an engaged woman is raped in town but doesn't scream loud enough to be heard, both she and her rapist are to be stoned. (She's OK if it happens in the country, because there's no one around to have helped her...) However, the most amazing command comes in verses 28-29, which deals with the penalty for raping a woman who is not yet engaged:

****

Deuteronomy 22:28-29 New International Version (NIV)

If a man happens to meet a virgin who is not pledged to be married and rapes her and they are discovered, he shall pay her father fifty shekels of silver. He must marry the young woman, for he has violated her. He can never divorce her as long as he lives.

****

I will simply repeat the commands as given in scripture: If a woman who is not yet engaged is raped, **his punishment is paying for and marrying his victim without the possibility of divorce**. Is that really the best a perfect, moral God could come up with in this scenario?

This is the kind of law I would expect from a barbaric bronze-age culture, but not from an all-loving, all-good God of the universe (if he existed).

Slavery and Human Dignity

Slavery is an accepted practice - even commanded practice - all throughout the Bible. Human dignity, as one would expect to find from an all-loving creator who loves each person so much as to number the hairs on every head? Not so much. Here's just one of many, many examples of the juxtaposition of those two:

****

Exodus 21:20-21 New International Version (NIV)

Anyone who beats their male or female slave with a rod must be punished if the slave dies as a direct result, but they are not to be punished if the slave recovers after a day or two, since the slave is their property.

****

Apologists will point out that this is actually a novel idea - punishment for killing a slave was relatively unheard of. Again, though, with the stroke of a pen God could have altered the course of human history by creating laws that dignified all humans, even abolishing slavery right then and there (not to mention fixing everything else that has been discussed thus far)! But he didn't. Once again, God's laws reflect the barbaric culture rather than reflecting an all-loving, all-good creator by any possible definition.

In the next post we'll continue to examine God's moral stances, this time on marriage and abortion.

****

This one hit a hot button on both sides of the issue. Supporters came out with statements like "I can only believe in a God who is MORE intelligent and MORE moral than I am" (a sentiment I would echo in a later post.) I found the Christian responses to such a clear immoral teaching to be fascinating, to say the least, even though they resembled what I would have likely said years ago.

> 1) The Law was given as a minimum standard to move a barbaric culture forward. He had no other choice given the environment. In that culture, the rape victim would be better off dead than being an unmarried woman with no heir. To interpret it through a modern American cultural lens is to be in error.
>
> Answer: So wait - your primary way of justifying this is that God "had" to make the laws this way? You're saying the he could not - with the stroke of the writer's pen - have imbued equality and human dignity, that these were the best laws he could come up with?
>
> I have some better examples:
>
>> A) Make the rapist work as a slave for the rest of his life to support the girl, no marriage required.
>>
>> B) For sure don't punish the rape victim in any circumstance.
>
> I propose that these two ideas - while they may not be perfect or complete in themselves - are far superior to what the God of the universe laid out for his people. Am I wrong?

Those laws (which are very representative of Biblical laws in general towards women) are obviously morally flawed. I am proposing that they reflect the ignorant misogynistic bronze-age culture of the day and in no way reflect a perfect moral being.

The culture that existed was the result of ignorant man in very early stages of moral evolution. The fact that the laws were what they were actually fits very nicely into my naturalist worldview, because they are man-made, with a supernatural being implied in order to give them more credibility than they deserved.

If you are to believe the Bible, that God is the same today as he was thousands of years ago, and is perfect and consistent throughout scripture, there's just no easy way out of this. Trust me - I tried and fought for years.

To your last point, if this passage is not for our culture, why do Christians try to apply the parts of it they happen to agree with or like to our culture today? Why not just write off the whole thing as inapplicable?

2) Those laws don't apply any more. Jesus and his death on the cross makes them null and void.

Answer: You and Jesus have a misunderstanding then:

Matthew 5:17-19 -- "Do not think that I have come to abolish the Law or the Prophets; I have not come to abolish them but to fulfill them. For truly I tell you, until heaven and earth disappear, not the smallest letter, not the least stroke of a pen, will by any means disappear from the Law until everything is accomplished. Therefore anyone who sets aside one of the least of these commands and teaches others accordingly will be called least in the kingdom of heaven, but whoever practices and teaches these commands will be called great in the kingdom of heaven."

Do you disagree, or do you really believe those who practice and teach all of the commands of the Law will really be the greatest in the kingdom of Heaven?

[There was no reply to this point.]

13 GOD ON MARRIAGE AND ABORTION

January 17th, 2014 (morning):

> This is the 13th installment in my deconversion series of posts. We'd like to give God a pass sometimes by claiming that the immoral laws in the Old Testament were somehow not directly from him. What do you do, then, when one of the worst offenders claims to be exactly that? This post examines a particularly odious command which claims to be the direct words of God with regards to trust issues in a marriage relationship. It also presents a pretty severe challenge to those who would claim that God and the Bible are "pro-life" with regards to abortion. You can argue with my interpretations of scripture, but if you believe the Bible is inerrant, are you willing to argue with Moses?

****

Morality Part 6: God on Marriage and Abortion

In the previous two post I discussed the standard the Bible forces us to use when judging God's morality: God and Jesus are one, God is the same throughout eternity, and the ministry of Jesus did exactly as he said in Matthew 5, and thus did not nullify the Old Testament law in the slightest sense - at least not from a moral standpoint. Using this lens, we will now examine several laws that pertain to marriage and abortion.

Marriage seminars based on "biblical concepts" are given every year in thousands of churches across the nation, and by and large, I think they do more good than harm. The only reason this is true, however, is because they don't cover all of what the Bible commands regarding marriage. For example:

****

Numbers 5:11-21   New International Version (NIV)

Then the Lord said to Moses, "Speak to the Israelites and say to them: 'If a man's wife goes astray and is unfaithful to him so that another man has sexual relations with her, and this is hidden from her **husband and her impurity is undetected** (since there is no witness against her and she has not been caught in the act), and if feelings of jealousy come over her husband and **he suspects his wife** and she is impure—**or if he is jealous and suspects her even though she is not impure** - then he is to take his wife to the priest [along with material for a jealousy offering.]

The priest shall bring her and have her stand before the Lord. Then he shall take some holy water in a clay jar and put some dust from the tabernacle floor into the water. After the priest has had the woman stand before the Lord, he shall loosen her hair and place in her hands the reminder-offering, the grain offering for jealousy, while he himself holds the bitter water that brings a curse. Then the priest shall put the woman under oath and say to her, "If no other man has had sexual relations with you and you have not gone astray and become impure while married to your husband, may this bitter water that brings a curse not harm you. But if you have gone astray while married to your husband and you have made yourself impure by having sexual relations with a man other than your husband" - here the priest is to put the woman under this curse - "may the Lord cause you to become a curse among your people when he makes your womb miscarry and your abdomen swell.

****

So a man suspects his wife of unfaithfulness and gets to drag her out before the religious leader, she has to drink a concoction[36] **designed to abort her baby**, and if her body physically reacts to this, she's deemed guilty and subject to punishment up to and including death? Anyone care to wager the percentage of false positives this ceremony produced? Is this the reflection

---

[36] Note that at the time this was written, man had no concept of germs and bacteria. Thus, the randomness of the drink causing sickness in some and not others may have been due to level of cleanliness of the floor. People in those days walked around in animal manure on the streets prior to walking into the tabernacle. Who knows what might be picked up off that floor?

of a God who is all-good and all-loving? Or is this a god that is created to reflect (and justify) the barbaric culture of the day?

Just as good when it comes to marriage are the verses in Deuteronomy 22: 13-21. In this passage, if a man isn't happy with his wife after their wedding night, he can claim that she was not a virgin when they first had sex. If the girl's parents are unable to produce a bloody sheet as proof of the existence of an intact hymen (never mind how they were to obtain this evidence), she is to be executed. Apparently the God of the universe never heard of situations where virgin intercourse produced no blood, or where a hymen was torn via innocent natural means prior to sexual activity. Apparently no one considered how the husband might have access to and dispose of evidence before a parent could get to it. How many innocents were killed in the name of this standard of morality?

****

I knew this would be the most difficult post on biblical morality, as it addressed one of the passages that had caused me the greatest cognitive dissonance as a believer. I considered this to be the final nail in the coffin of "perfect" Biblical morality from a fundamentalist perspective. Apologists (like I was) often try to downplay this and other Old Testament atrocities as being whitewashed or nullified by Jesus, but I eventually realized that Matthew 5:17-19 doesn't give them (me) the option to believe that. Some will also try to separate Old Testament laws by ceremonial vs. moral (or other distinction) as a way to carve out those parts they find hard to stomach. In this case, however, the Bible explicitly called this out as a direct command of God, which makes it harder to get away from by relabeling it. It also hit upon two key issues - women's rights in marriage and abortion - that most fundamentalist Christians would struggle with in this context. My fundamentalist Facebook friends had no response. I continued to ask for feedback on this post and passage of scripture for several days, with promises from some that they would get to it. The responses, as of this printing, never came.

14 HUMANIST MORALITY VS. BIBLICAL MORALITY

January 17, 2014 (afternoon):

This is the 14th installment in my deconversion series of posts, and my second one for the day. In the past several posts I have provided an answer to those who have claimed that "without God there can be no morality" by showing that natural selection does provide a possible explanation for it as well as by demonstrating that the Bible has some serious problems in terms of the morality of the God it portrays. In this final summary of our first pass at the morality topic, I will present a side-by-side comparison of Biblical morality - based on the Bible - with Humanist morality based on the Platinum Rule. My goal is to represent each side fairly, both positive and negative, and allow you to determine for yourself which moral worldview is superior and which one more closely lines up to your own personal sense of right and wrong.

****

Morality Part 7: Humanist Morality vs. Biblical Morality

Throughout the whole morality miniseries I have had two goals: answer the objection "If God doesn't exist, where does morality come from?" and expose true "Biblical morality" in areas where it is clearly inferior to the moral standards of most believers. Let's take a quick look at the two moral worldviews side by side, evaluate their basis for making moral decisions, and apply them to controversial issues today (I can do deeper dives into these if comments indicate it necessary) and see how the different moral standards end up treating individuals.

Comparison Point	Bible	Humanism
Basis for morality	Sets of sometimes conflicting rules given to man by a supernatural being.	Scientifically-based long-term view of natural consequences, codified via the "Platinum Rule."
How to Evaluate Issues and Situations	Depending on the issue, can vary based on which scriptures one chooses to apply directly and which ones to ignore or reframe.	Can vary based on understanding (or misunderstanding) of what the other entity in any exchange would want out of the situation, and allows for gray area in some situations.
Example: Homosexuality	Condemned as evil and immoral (sinful). Punishments up to and including death.	Recognized as having a natural and genetic basis.. Platinum rule demands equal treatment and respect.
Example: Abortion	Depends on which verses are being used. In some scriptures, is used as a punishment or even commanded by God. In others, God seems to reflect the modern pro-life viewpoint.	Depends on when scientifically defensible human life begins. General consensus is around 20-week mark of pregnancy when brainwaves develop. Prior to this point, no moral conflict.
Example: Slavery	Most of the Bible seems to accept it, although views on how slaves should be treated evolve from Old to New Testament.	Platinum rule leaves no room for slavery in any form, as no one is likely to ever wish they were a slave in a given transaction.

Example: Capital Punishment	Bible clearly allows and calls for it, often in cases involving non-capital crimes by today's standards (for example, a woman having sex before marriage, blasphemy, etc.)	Gray area. Platinum rule would have to be outweighed by overall effects of Nash Equilibrium in given circumstances, so justification would have to be extreme risk to society if not implemented.
Example: Spanking as Discipline	Clearly calls for hitting children as disciplinary method.	Allows use of better modern scientific knowledge regarding behavior management, positive reinforcement, etc. and recognizes that hitting a child in **most** cases is both harmful and ineffective in producing desired behavior.
Example: Gender Equality	In vast majority of scriptures, women are at best seen as subservient to men, and at worst as outright property of their fathers or husbands.	Platinum rule demands equal treatment and respect regardless of gender.
Example: Polygamy	Depends on which verses are being applied or which examples are being followed. In some cases, men commanded to be husband of one wife. In others, implied command is to take another wife, regardless of existing marital status.	Gray area. Prohibiting polygamy for individuals that wish to participate in that lifestyle seems to violate Platinum Rule, however arguments can be made for overall damage to society if allowed. Needs further study and evaluation.

When you look at real-life, difficult decisions with regards to deciding how we are going to treat each other and what moral impositions we place on each other by force of law, I believe it becomes clear that attempting to apply the Platinum Rule **on its own** produces a better, less ambiguous moral code than attempts to follow misguided or conflicting Biblical rules. It's not always perfect or clear, but it is in every case I can think of superior.

I propose that you may have chosen to attribute your moral behavior to some promise of reward in Heaven or avoidance of punishment in Hell, but in reality you are moral because of who you are at the deepest genetic level and due to environment in which you grew up. You possess an innate understanding of the effects of moral behaviors on producing stronger societies, better relationships, and better personal outcomes in the long run. Remove your belief in the supernatural, and you'd still be the same moral person you are today. Your views on some issues might necessarily change for the better, but your general goodness and kindness would be unaffected.

Put another way, you should now have a clear, full understanding of what "God-given, biblical" morality actually means, and be able to measure it against your own moral code and behavior. Now compare your own innate sense of right and wrong with a Humanist moral code based on the Platinum Rule. Which worldview better describes and predicts the way you actually think when making moral decisions?

The final conclusion, of course, is up to you. For me, it is obvious that I never did buy into the complete Biblical stance on morality since it often clearly requires taking an immoral position. At the end of my faith journey, I found that when I evaluated Humanist morality, it was in essence what I was already practicing, simply without the unnecessary supernatural extras.

For more on Humanism and the basis for Humanist morals, check out the latest iteration of the Humanist Manifesto (approximately one page):

http://americanhumanist.org/Humanism/Humanist_Manifesto_III

For additional, in-depth discussions on morality check out these videos (13 and 17 minutes, respectively):

http://www.youtube.com/watch?v=T7xt5LtgsxQ

http://www.youtube.com/watch?v=sN-yLH4bXAI

****

There were some replies to this post, but they were primarily rehashes of "I believe God did it" comments from previous posts. I knew this would be a contentious post and, as I expected, Christians really bristled when I compared Biblical morality with Humanist morality side by side. Many even agreed with my logic, just not my conclusions. Frankly, I was happy that folks were wrestling with the issues at all considering the intense challenges to their faith they presented.

Based on some of the "I believe" type responses, I challenged my fundamentalist friends with the following question:

> "What evidence, if it existed, would it take to convince you that you were wrong on any or all of those views? Have you ever considered the possibility you might be wrong, and what you would need to see/hear/learn in order to be able to abandon what you believe?"

This question generated much discussion, but no one was willing to throw out an answer. Instead, some tried to shift to "Why are you trying so hard to convince me that I'm wrong?" as though challenging their beliefs was somehow an immoral act on my part. I tried to explain to them that my only interest was in seeking truth, an in pushing on their beliefs I was openly inviting them to push on mine. Engagement in the conversation was voluntary, but if questions were asked or positions were stated, I felt they deserved answers and - if applicable - holes poked in their underlying assumptions. I tried to convey that it was a sign of respect that I was willing to engage with them, and it was. I hope that message came through.

15 PERSONAL EXPERIENCE

January 18th, 2014:

> This is the 15th installment in my deconversion series of posts. When "inerrant Bible" Christians like I was are confronted with stark examples of either moral or academic error in scripture, we often fall back on personal experience. "I know God exists because of X miracle I have witnessed, or Y experience that has to be of supernatural origin." In this post I will examine those claims - just like the ones I made as a believer - and why I eventually abandoned them as justifications for belief.

****

<u>Why Personal Experience Fails as Proof of the Existence of God</u>

When I was a believer, I was an ardent defender of God's existence through what I called his "fingerprints" in my life - personal experiences and events that, had they gone another way, would have drastically changed my life today (with the expectation that it would have been worse). I had many, many personal experiences during worship services and prayer. I even had what I thought was supernatural foresight that I attributed to the influence of the Holy Spirit in my life, and I wasn't shy about telling folks about all of these proofs for God.

Since my deconversion then, many who have had and continue to have similar experiences want to know how I can simply throw all of that away and claim to no longer believe in the supernatural. And the honest truth is I still experience sensations that I used to attribute to "the movement of the Holy Spirit" or similar Christian terms. Interestingly enough, I often experience these feelings in church settings, or while listening to worship music (which I still do from time to time). How then, can I still be an atheist?

My experience is not unusual for those who have deconverted from faith. Folks from more charismatic backgrounds than mine who have deconverted still find themselves speaking in tongues from time to time! The reality is that these kinds of emotional responses are part of being human, regardless of one's belief system. Some metaphysicists refer to the sensation as universal vibration or enlightenment. Some members of decidedly non-Christian faith systems actually train themselves to go several steps beyond and actually enter an altered state of consciousness so that they can commune with the eternal on a personal level. Plain old psychology can give us the same kinds of experiences and sensations with concepts of personal alignment, hypnosis, and unconditional positive regard in a therapeutic setting. And I get the exact same feelings listening to some Coldplay music that I get when listening to Christian songs that still move me.

Part of my deconversion came when I was pressed on what made my experiences any different or superior to those of folks from other faiths. I was forced to step back and admit that there was no objective way to separate these biologically identical experiences, so I stopped basing my evaluation on subjective experiences. What I felt could be replicated in a lab or nearly any other religion on earth, as well as many emotionally driven but non-religious environments. Situations and "miracles" could be explained in any number of natural ways. Foreknowledge was just good guessing and luck, when it was right (and it wasn't always). What was true, however, could be objectively quantified and known, without risk of subjective experiences and confirmation bias. Thus I do not and will not use my personal experiences as a deciding factor if I am to believe there is anything to the existence of the supernatural.

What is intriguing is that I am finding in my discussions since coming out as an atheist that people of faith base their beliefs on personal experiences and feelings rather than objective sources of truth. The "Bible as home base" is for many people a familiar phrase, but not something they actually believe. They tend to reject the same biblical stories that I do, but then have no problem still believing in "Jesus." What they actually worship is not the God of the Bible, as revealed in the Bible, but some idealization of what they believe an all-knowing, all-loving, all-powerful God would be like. They simply play mental gymnastics with problematic New Testament teachings like Matthew 5:17-19, in which Jesus explicitly states that you cannot do what they do and follow him. They have a sense that the Bible's views on things like homosexuality are off, but "God is God, so who am I to argue?" (Which is interesting, given how they can discard Matthew 5 and other significant chunks of their holy book…)

Often, then, these folks will fall back on personal stories (just like I did): unverifiable miracles and healings; strong personal impressions of God's leading and how it all worked out for them; etc. The stories and testimonies of my Christian friends are identical in nature and substance across almost any faith, including New Age, Hinduism, Buddhism, and Islam, which represent ideologically incompatible systems of belief. Thus they cancel out and I believe deserve very little weight when personally determining what is real and true.

****

The discussion here was muted compared to the morality miniseries, but there were some points of contention.

> 1) Is personal experience that can't be explained proof of any specific religion? No. However, it shouldn't be ignored either, when there is no explanation.
>
> Answer: I get it. The question for me became this: was there a natural explanation for any of the personal experiences I had that seemed to be otherwise? If I examined really closely, in **all** cases I could come up with a plausible natural explanation, even if it seemed improbable. Thus the trick in getting past personal experience is trying to weed out what you want to be true from what you actually observed and looking at it with an objective eye. It's hard to do.

A couple of folks recommended Daniel Kahneman's book *Thinking Fast and Slow*[37] as a way to think about interpreting seemingly religious experiences. I have not read the book, but based on the individuals that recommended it, I suspect it does a great job of breaking this issue down.

---

[37] http://www.amazon.com/Thinking-Fast-Slow-Daniel-Kahneman-ebook/dp/B00555X8OA

16 MY PATH TO ATHEISM

January 19th, 2014:

This is the 16th installment in my deconversion series of posts. In the morality mini-series, I was pretty tough on an earlier version of my fundamentalist faith, however it is true that I did not immediately jump from fundamentalism to atheism. This post goes into more detail as to the phases of my journey over time, and why I eventually gave up the idea of belief in the supernatural and became an atheist.

****

My Path to Atheism

In this series I have been pretty hard on religion thus far - in part because it took a lot of hard thinking to move me from fundamentalism to a more moderate Christianity, then to Deism before finally submitting to atheism. In this post I will detail that journey and explain where I can see religion doing good, and under what conditions.

Fundamentalism requires belief in an inerrant Bible. There are several ways one can get to error. Just a few of them: mistakes in the texts that implicate credibility (for example, logistics involved in getting 3 million people and everything they carried with them across the Red Sea in one night...), inconsistencies in important teachings that cannot be resolved in an intellectually honest way (as in the morality passages I have discussed), or downright factual errors attributed to an omniscient God that - if he truly existed - would not have been made. The journey away from fundamentalism is a short one. One single, clear error is enough to crack the foundations of a fundamentalist worldview, and the Bible contains more than enough material along these lines to cause a serious student of scripture to reject Biblical inerrancy.

The next step, however, is usually not atheism (although it sometimes is - it just wasn't for me.) When I lost faith in Biblical inerrancy, I still valued much of what the Bible taught and chose to filter the problems through a lens of "progressive revelation" - meaning I was able to attempt to filter the terrible stories and laws through a worldview that said God gave his revelation cyclically, and later messengers had a more complete/accurate view of God than Moses would have (for example). Sure, there are problems with that worldview - logically, couldn't one just say that as the culture naturally evolved, so did their concept of a supernatural being? But it's still a logical next stop from fundamentalism.

Where moderate Christianity starts to fall apart is in the examination of even the latest writers and their own set of problems. Jesus is recorded to have said things that would have been clearly understood by the people around him, but turned out to be untrue[38], and so mental gymnastics exercises are engaged to rectify them. (Yes, they can be rectified, but it's a stretch.) Many statements of his regarding what believers would be able to do by the power of faith alone[39] have been tested and found lacking for thousands of years, except for the charlatans on TV and their "miracles" - the unverified kind - which are then used as a template by which other Christians can interpret events in their lives as miracles too. *sigh*

The implication that God's progressive revelation ended with the writings of the New Testament is problematic as well. Paul, for example, codified gender inequality to some extent[40], but even worse, proliferated the Old Testament idea that homosexuality was an affront to God[41]. When one applies the golden or Platinum Rule to either of these teaching, they are obviously immoral by a consistent application of morality. And yet, we are told that they represent the final revelation, and as such, even moderate Christians who eschew Biblical inerrancy will still sorrowfully move into the "love the sinner, hate the sin" category and vote against treating their homosexual brothers and sisters as equal people with equal rights due to their inability to disobey God's word. If, however, one continues to press on these issues, a common conclusion to reach is to abandon Paul as inspired.[42] Then, only after much soul-searching and examination, we can admit that the Jesus of the Bible was probably not reflective of the actual

---

[38] For example, see Matthew 24:29-34, Matthew 16:28, and Matthew 10:23.
[39] See Mark 11:23-24
[40] See 1 Corinthians 14:34
[41] See Romans 1:24-27
[42] http://www.religioustolerance.org/inerrant0.htm

Jesus who might have lived, but rather a legendary view that imbued him with powers that he likely never had nor claimed to have in the first place.[43]

At the culmination of this journey, however, I could still hold on to basic precepts of the Bible and faith in the supernatural through a belief system that was just a step above Deism. Deism is the belief that a supernatural force was responsible for the creation of the universe, but has not and does not intervene since that time. A "slightly spiritual" Deist (which is really a contradiction of terms) like I was could say that this force or being intervened from time to time, or perhaps influenced key events in order to produce a certain outcome, but was not involved in the day-to-day lives of each human being. Thus, one who concedes to the evidence of evolution via natural selection can still imply that something must have stepped in at some point to make us the way we are.

What finally pushed me over the line into full-blown atheism was the study of economic theory (which allowed me to figure out a realistic basis for the evident morality in our world that needed no supernatural explanation) and quantum physics (which allowed me to figure out a realistic basis for the existence of the universe that needed no supernatural explanation.) When I reached that point, I had a choice to make. I could either continue to believe in the supernatural, or I could not. In every case, believing in the supernatural meant agreeing with everything that my naturalist worldview said, plus God. In the end, I had to concede that God or any other supernatural force was simply not necessary to explain anything in our world. One could still choose to add belief in him if one chose, but doing so was at this point a conscious act of addition without a clear purpose other than to appease family and friends. I then left my faith to Occam's Razor[44]: if I had two competing theories that both explained equally well the things I was evaluating, I should prefer the simpler of the two. If light + prisms + fairies did no better in explaining rainbows than simply light + prisms, my fairy hypothesis needed to be discarded. Thus, I realized I was an atheist, and probably really had been for a while before I was willing to admit it to myself.

Please note: While I necessarily can never move back to fundamentalism, and probably not even a belief in the Bible's representation of a historical Jesus, I am by all means open to new evidence that might prove the existence of God or the supernatural. If I were to be visited by a supernatural being in the presence of witnesses who saw and heard the

---

[43] http://en.wikipedia.org/wiki/Christ_myth_theory
[44] http://simple.wikipedia.org/wiki/Occam's_razor

same thing, I would have to reconsider. If every naturalistic explanation for the existence of the universe is proven false, I will be forced to reconsider my stance on creation ex nihilo[45]. I'm not anti-God, and in fact, would welcome clear evidence of the existence of the supernatural into my worldview. Until such evidence appears, however, I am forced to assent to the best evidence I have available now, and that evidence clearly points to a lack of need for belief in the supernatural.

****

This represented the intellectual side of my atheist "testimony." Christian responses did not specifically address the issues I laid out, but continued to try to get me to see God in different ways.

1) You can't demand God show you himself in physical form. You have to look internally for him.

Answer: If I have to look internally for him, how am I supposed to tell the difference between a real supernatural being and an active imagination?

2) Take away everything that prevents you from finding God. Examine your own motives, and then simply pray that He removes the things that keep you from Him.

Answer: It's not that simple. Human beings tend to find the will of God through "nudging" or whatever you want to call it, but it predictably follows what that person really wants significantly more often than not. And when not, it's often an unhealthy emotional decision coming from a place of guilt or fear... I could write a book on that alone.

I propose that if God exists, then because of the conflicting stories and often inferior outcomes, we have no way to determine whether that which we want to be his voice is actually it, or just ourselves creating a voice to fill in for the God who will not speak clearly. I also contend that no matter what the outcome, we either give God credit because it worked out, or let him off the hook and take the blame if it didn't because it's then that we realize we were acting out of self-interest rather than God's will. The game is rigged.

---

[45] http://en.wikipedia.org/wiki/Ex_nihilo

17 DESIRE FOR BELIEF

January 20th, 2014:

This is the 17th installment in my deconversion series of posts. It's a longer post, which addresses what I personally feel is something extremely important for my critics to understand.

As some have pointed out on my behalf, there were no ulterior motives for my move to atheism other than a search for truth. In fact, I knew I'd have a lot to lose by changing to this system of belief. I have already detailed many of the reasons I felt I had to leave the faith. In this post I briefly detail my personal history with faith and desire to believe from my early teens into my early 30's, as well as explain why I eventually abandoned that line of reasoning. I will leave it up to you to decide whether my faith was the real deal or not.

****

The Siren Song of Faith and Desire for Belief

No One Wanted God to Be Real More Than I Did

I grew up in a rural, lower-class (economically speaking), fundamentalist family. I grew up with a firm belief in God, the inerrancy of scripture, and the fact the God speaks directly to anyone who has a heart to listen. I had a lot of great reasons for wanting God to be real:

- I was about as socially awkward as you can get without having an official diagnosis on the autism spectrum (and some might argue that I should have one, but I digress…),

- I lived in a broken home where the relationship between my divorced parents was so hostile and other circumstances so twisted my dad did not talk to us for nearly a decade,
- I was physically and emotionally abused in that decade by my step-father,
- I was physically smaller than most boys my age for a long time, suffered from a weight problem, and had acne so bad my face was more pimple than skin at times, and
- as a result I was a consistent target for bullies, and was often desperately lonely.

When someone tries to tell me that I simply don't want to believe in God - an invisible but ever-watching and all-powerful friend who loves me like the perfect father, protects me, and wants to lead me down a life path of joy and fulfillment as part of an overarching plan for my life - my reactions range from delirious laughter to burning anger. If there was ever a poster boy for someone who needed to believe in God in order to have a reason to wake up the next morning and face what was going to come at him that day, it was me.

Trying to Hear the Voice of God

I desperately wanted God's protection and guidance in my life. I would pray, and agonize, and wait for a response that never came. Years in my mid-teens would often find me at the church (I had a key, I was there so much and involved in so many things…) walking around the building, talking to God, asking him why my life was the way it was, praying, crying, begging, etc. Nothing. I would claim[46] Bible verses on faith, and so fully believed they were going to come true that I made some idiotic decisions based on them. Then, like a good little Christian, I would try to let God off the hook and blame myself for not being faithful enough when it did not come about as promised. I had plenty of reasons to question whether the Bible was true, and were it not for the discovery of Norm Geisler's book *When Skeptics Ask*[47], I likely would have. His logic, and in particular the cosmological argument for the existence of God, was enough to convince me that God was necessary to explain existence, and if he did exist, then

---

[46] A faith act borrowed from prosperity theologies that included reading a scripture out loud, claiming to believe it was true for my life, and then purposefully making decisions as though that promise would come true regardless of the circumstances.

[47] http://www.amazon.com/When-Skeptics-Ask-Christian-Evidences/dp/0801014980/

Christianity was the only religion in the world that was internally logically consistent enough to possibly be true. Why, then, was my life so screwed up and God so silent?

Then it occurred to me - at the ripe old age of 16: What if I'm looking for the wrong things, or listening with the wrong kinds of ears? What if, instead of speaking directly and giving clear guidance God was sending me messages through events and people in my life? So I started paying attention using that framework, and suddenly the messages started coming if I just looked hard enough.

Getting the Messages

One spring afternoon I remember well, I was the last person to leave the school building (which frequently happened - I didn't really rush to get home). One of my frequent bullies drove up, saw I was alone, and raced to get between me and my car. He jumped out of his truck and got up in my face (he was a good deal bigger than I was) and threatened me, begging me to give him a reason to beat the shit out of me. (Direct quote.) I was scared, but at a point in my life where I wasn't afraid to die for a cause. I threw down my book bag, looked him in the eye, and said "Leon, you do what you have to do, but I won't stop being who I am and I won't stop telling people God loves them. He loves you, and if it takes you beating me up or killing me for you to see that, then do your worst."

Ever seen those videos where a grizzly bear back down from a barking dachshund? Well, that's exactly what happened. Leon got back in his truck and drove away, telling me to stay out of his way, with me shouting after him that I couldn't do it because God and I loved him too much. I felt like Elisha in 2 Kings chapter 6, and could almost feel myself surrounded by those fiery chariots. People in my church were amazed by the story. A couple of months later, Leon - who was a reckless driver and teenage drinker - was killed in a one-vehicle car accident. I was initially crushed, because I knew I had failed to reach him and he was now doomed for eternity in Hell. Could I have done more to save him, I wondered? At the same time, I wondered if God was sending me a message: "Don't worry about those who threaten you. I'm taking care of you." It was a powerful and fearful thing to consider.

Breaking the Code

In the movie *A Beautiful Mind*[48], John Nash (the guy who posited the Nash Equilibrium that serves as the basis for my theory on naturalist morality) is shown being asked by the U.S. government to look for secret codes in newspapers and other everyday media. He's brilliant, and when he looks for patterns and secret messages, he finds them, and drops them off at various safe houses as directed by his contact. We learn later, however, that none of this is real, and his brain has constructed the contact and several other characters. So while he was doing very real, very valuable work in economic theory, he was also spending significant time divining patterns and messages in secret codes that simply did not exist.

I'm no John Nash, but I understand the power of the delusion he followed, and how easy it is for someone to get sucked into believing their own stuff - even to the point of believing you have super powers. I was reading books on parenting by my early teens, and as a result had more formal knowledge on how parenting choices affected childhood outcomes than most of the adults in my community. I was reading marriage and relationship books by the time I could drive, and could see unhealthy aspects of the relationships in which I found myself connected in some way. I became fascinated with trying to evaluate life situations and divining God's will in them, and with my intellectual bent and intentional study, I became really adept at figuring out what was going to happen to people long before things became a reality.

Sometimes, looking back, my predictions were simply a result of my study of human nature and relationships. I remember vividly arguing with a family member when I was 14 years old about the way they were raising their child. I told them if they continued to allow certain types of behavior that this person would grow up and end up in prison someday. I was berated and told to mind my own business. A few years later, to everyone's shock but mine, my prediction came true. (That story has a happy ending and a life that has been turned around completely, I'm happy to say.) I had already come to the conclusion that I had the gift of prophecy and foreknowledge, and this was a major confirmation of that reality.

Other times things would happen and I would make educated guesses that would be close enough to right that I (and others around me) would claim supernatural influence. For example, with our first baby, my wife and I could pretty much pinpoint the day of conception (for reasons that don't

---

[48] http://www.amazon.com/Beautiful-Mind-Russell-Crowe/dp/B00ENYKBD0/

matter for this discussion…) Given a normal human gestation period, our baby was going to be born around December 12th. My wife had blood pressure problems early in the pregnancy, so I was not confident that we would go the full 40 weeks. Later, however, a doctor gave us a due date based on an ultrasound of around December 19th. My wife was convinced by the doctor, but I had serious doubts - so much, in fact, that I said with a wink and a smile, "Nah, she'll be born on December 9th." Being a cocky little S.O.B., I continued to stand firm on my claim for weeks to come. No way was that baby going till the 19th. Sure enough, on the morning of December 9th, my wife called me to tell me that the doctor had decided to induce labor due to the blood pressure and related potential health issues associated with waiting. While my daughter was actually born on the 10th, we did go to the doctor on the 9th and start inducing labor. Creepy, right? Another prophecy fulfilled.

I have lots of smaller-impact events that I could point to, but in the end, most of it really just boiled down to being fairly smart and training myself to be able to read situations and predict outcomes. Today I would call that strategic thinking, not prophecy. And indeed, if I had truly been a prophet, I would have never been wrong. However, I was. It turned out my ability to predict hinged greatly on how well I knew all of the variables in a situation. Whenever I would predict something right, I would claim supernatural influence. Whenever I was wrong, I would wonder about it, but figure that I simply must have nudged myself rather than gotten an actual nudge from God.

Finding the "Fingerprints of God"

Along these lines, I would also point to other things in my life and explain how supernatural forces were the only possible explanation. My high score on a standardized test could only be explained by supernatural influence. God would set up situations that would lead me to romantic relationships - which, for a kid like me, was nothing to sneeze at! A beloved pastor would be under political attack (which in small, Southern Baptist churches, happens a lot and can quickly cost a pastor his livelihood), but God would help my grandpa get an even bigger group of people to out-vote them and protect his man. I hit a deer driving down a country road on the way to a weekend Revival Teams meeting and God provided a guy in the church who could fix my car and get me home. Etc.

This did not stop in my teens. I kept looking at the world through this lens until well into my 30's. God would lead me to invest in a small startup business, and it would fail, but things learned in that opportunity would lead me to even greater opportunities and jobs, and so it was all part of some master plan to get me from point A to point B. (It wasn't until much later that God finally figured out that an MBA might have helped.) Sure my son had autism, but God had also made him brilliant, so his recovery could serve as a model for other families to follow. Everything, good or bad, had an ultimate purpose, and I just needed to be smart enough to recognize it.

It really irritates me when people claim that since I'm now an atheist, I never really was a true believer. I daresay I was more of a believer than most who would criticize me today. I was sold on Jesus in more, and more personal ways, than most folks ever will be.

A Beautiful Lie

My fatal personality flaw with regards to my faith was being brutally honest with myself. I have already detailed some of the things that led me to finally conclude that neither God nor anything else supernatural actually exists. At some point I realized I had to decide which road to take: believing a beautiful lie that made my life easier, or a hard truth that made me better. I could take a light + prisms + fairies approach to explain rainbows, or I could be honest and say that fairies weren't a necessary part of the equation.

Many of the responses to my coming out posts seem rooted in fear of what the responders will lose if they stop believing what they believe. What if there's no heaven? No final justice or reward? What if there is no absolute standard of right and wrong, no moral lawgiver? What if there is no ultimate meaning to our lives? And for some, the prospect of losing this construct of reality is too great to even consider the possibility that it might all be invention and myth. Some would rather believe a beautiful lie than face a cold, hard truth. And I really, really, really get it.

For me, however, it was more important to uncover what was true, to the degree that truth could be discerned, even if that meant giving up a significant degree of certainty and comfort embedded in the lies that I believed. The siren song of faith was not enough to keep me from examining evidence and questioning what I believed to be true. Even if it meant looking back at decades of powerful personal experiences and recasting them in a light of statistical probability plus a little dumb luck, I

71

was willing to do it to find truth. Unexpectedly, I learned that my fears were wrong, and a new life of freedom and joy found in being an authentic human being was discovered.

Early on in this deconversion series, someone asked a very valid question: Why not continue believing a lie, even if you realize it probably is? I had a good life for 30+ years based on that lie, so why mess up a good thing? At some point, I will post an answer to that question, knowing the price I would pay as a result of going public with my changed world view. For this post, the main thing you have to walk away with is that there was never anyone who wanted to believe in a loving God more than I did, and I had plenty of direct personal experiences to back up my belief. You can fairly criticize me for many things, but a lack of "real" faith or desire to believe is ridiculous.

****

Christians came out guns blazing to this one. Apparently they didn't care much about my intellectual testimony, but the story of my social/emotional departure from faith was too much to bear. One relative even let me know she was blocking me from her Facebook wall because reading this was too painful, and wondered out loud about my marriage because if her husband were to turn from his faith, she would feel more betrayed than if he had cheated on her. Fortunately, I have and will continue to take great care of my marriage relationship, so her concerns were unfounded.

It was interesting to note that at this point I started to receive criticism from what I call "fundamentalist atheists" for my approach in coming out. They felt that ridicule is a better tool than reason for creating change, and that my Humanist "be nice to everyone"[49] approach lacked courage and authenticity. They tended to either prefer a Hedonist "ends justify the means"[50] strategy, or took a Nihilist "there is no point to any of this"[51] approach, thus excusing their treatment of those who disagreed with them. I simply took this to show that people are people, and no matter what belief system you move to, you'll always have zealots to contend with when you get there.

---

[49] http://americanhumanist.org/Humanism/Humanist_Manifesto_III
[50] http://en.wikipedia.org/wiki/Consequentialism
[51] http://en.wikipedia.org/wiki/Nihilism

18 WHAT IF I'M WRONG?

January 21st, 2014:

> This is the 18th installment in my deconversion series of posts. So far the most significant comeback my fundamentalist Christians have given for the folly in my journey is the "What if you're wrong?" question, with the implication being eternal damnation and potentially infecting my loved ones with a similar eternal fate should they follow my path. In this post, I lay out why I think such fears are ridiculous, and why I'm not worried about my eternal destiny, even if I'm wrong and God does exist.

****

Why I'm Not Worried Even If I'm Wrong

I see no evidence to believe in the supernatural in any form: God, angels, demons, Heaven, Hell, crystals, psychic powers, mystical forces, etc. I am fully aware that there is a possibility that I could be wrong. Before choosing the path of honesty, I gave great thought to this, since "Hell is the wrong thing to be wrong about."[52] :) What I eventually concluded, however, was that even if I am wrong, there is nothing for me, nor anyone else who legitimately seeks truth, to fear.

God, if He Exists, is Not a Thug

The God of the Old Testament (and to a lesser extent, even the New Testament in places) comes across as a brutish, childish, misogynistic, racist thug with little regard for human life. He is an overlord dictator who rules with an iron fist and threatens any who dare question any of his diktats. His

---

[52] A relatively popular phrase among evangelical fundamentalists.

punishments are often far out of line with the supposed crimes being committed, his standards are unrealistic, and he often contradicts himself. Frankly, even if that god did exist, he wouldn't be a being worth serving.

On the other hand, if we accept the idea that God is at least as mature, loving, intelligent, caring, fair, and honest as the best of humanity, a very different picture emerges. I have to believe if a perfect being exists, he is at least as moral and loving as I am towards my wife and children.

My children are sometimes disobedient, disagreeable, and lack discernment. Sometimes they disagree with me in substantial ways, and sometimes that disagreement is based on a lack of self-awareness or a degree of immaturity that I know is a natural part of the learning and growing process. I cannot fathom picking a two-year time period in their lives - say, early teens - and, based on their lack of complete obedience or agreement with my every statement, locking them in a rat-infested prison cell in our basement for the next 30 years. How much more ridiculous is it, really, to think about an eternal, all-knowing being who creates every person and loves us deeply to be unable (really? something he cannot do?) to allow us to spend eternity with him based on human immaturity, lack of awareness, or simple stubbornness over the course of our tiny sliver of life on this planet? How much more ridiculous is it to imagine - based on our immaturity and lack of perfect knowledge - that he would doom us to eternal torment equivalent with eternal fire? Seriously folks, if that's God's love, then I love my children more than he loves me by a long shot. If he exists, I don't buy it, and I don't care what any holy book says. God's love is either perfect and superior to anything we can fathom in human nature, or he doesn't exist at all (or, again, he's not worth serving in the first place).

God, if He Exists, is Not Afraid of Questions or Discovery

My journey away from faith was a search for truth, and at the time I was confident that truth would lead me right back to the God I started with. If God is real, he's not afraid of hard questions, or objective evaluation of data, or scientific exploration, or new ideas, or human progress. He would embrace it! I can't imagine trying to stop my kids from going to middle or high school for fear they would get too smart and start disagreeing with me, or stop them from exploring ideas that differ from mine in an honest, open search for what is really true. Again, any God who would punish me for my journey and the conclusions to which I have come based on the data that I have examined would be a childish, insecure thug, and I would actively oppose the imposition of his will on humanity. However, if God does exist, his perfect nature would mean he would honor the intention behind my search for truth rather than punish me for coming to the wrong conclusion based on brutally honest evaluation.

God, if He Exists, is Just

Fundamentalist Christians have this idea of a magic spell - a prayer that can be said on one's deathbed that releases even the most evil person that ever lived from any eternal consequences and grants them access to Heaven. On the other hand, if said spell is not uttered, even the most moral Shaolin monk who spends his life in service of the suffering is doomed for eternal torture. "The only sin that leads to Hell is rejecting Christ," so they say.

What utter nonsense.

If God exists, his judgment must be based on intention and ability (which is based on genetics and environmental background) rather than outcomes. Even C.S. Lewis agrees with me on this point.

> "The bad psychological material is not a sin but a disease. It does not need to be repented of, but to be cured. And by the way, that is very important. Human beings judge one another by their external actions. God judges them by their moral choices. When a neurotic who has a pathological horror of cats forces himself to pick up a cat for some good reason, it is quite possible that in God's eyes he has shown more courage than a healthy man may have shown in winning the V.C. When a man who has been perverted from his youth and taught that cruelty is the right thing does some tiny little kindness, or refrains from some cruelty he might have committed, and thereby, perhaps, risks being sneered at by his companions, he may, in God's eyes, be doing more than you and I would do if we gave up life itself for a friend.
>
> It is as well to put this the other way round. Some of us who seem quite nice people may, in fact, have made so little use of a good heredity and good upbringing that we are really worse than those whom we regard as fiends. Can we be quite certain how we should have behaved if we had been saddled with the psychological outfit, and then with the bad upbringing, and then with the power, say, of Himmler? That is why Christians are told not to judge. We see only the results which a man's choices make out of his raw material. But God does not judge him on the raw material at all, but on what he has done with it. Most of the man's psychological makeup is probably due

> to his body: when his body dies all that will fall off him, and the real central man, the thing that chose, that made the best or worst out of this material, will stand naked. All sorts of nice things which we thought our own, but which were really due to a good digestion, will fall off some of us: all sorts of nasty things which were due to complexes or bad health will fall off others. We shall then, for the first time, see every one as he really was. There will be surprises."[53]

Thus, even if I am wrong, I can trust that my wrongness will be judged by a perfect, loving God who will judge me for my intentions and ability rather than outcomes. I am completely confident in standing before such a God and stating that I did my honest best with what I was given, and can trust that my eternal fate - if I have one - will be judged accordingly. I have nothing to fear.

****

Christian response to this was muted. One of my weapons in any debate with them is to be the kind of atheist they can't imagine God would send to Hell, and as such, they are put into a moral bind. The fact that they can't argue with my reasoning just makes it all the worse.

In this case, it was an agnostic friend who came up with the strongest criticisms.

> 1) If the spirit of the Bible is correct, God sets the rules. If we end up burning in Hell, it's not going to be much consolation that we "did our best".
>
> Answer: I've already laid out why I don't trust what the Bible says about God. And keep in mind, Christians argue that God is good (all the time), and that's why they serve him. We can have the discussion about what the appropriate response would be if God really was an insecure, childish, abusive thug if you want (if the Bible is accurate) but that's not the picture of God that anyone in the discussion is defending as far as I know.

---

[53] C.S. Lewis, Mere Christianity. http://www.goodreads.com/quotes/482608-the-bad-psychological-material-is-not-a-sin-but-a

2) But if when we die we're asked: "Were you taught the rules? Were you aware that the punishment for disobedience was eternal torment?" "I couldn't believe you'd really be so barbaric" probably won't cut it.

Answer: But that argument goes back to one of the criticisms of Pascal's Wager: which God do we believe in? There are lots of them, and they all promise eternal suffering for disobedience. If the Bible was more reliable and didn't contain such stark contradictions in character, it would have a leg up. As it stands, it's no more likely to be true than the Quran, Book of Mormon, Hinduism, or ancient Greek, Roman, or Norse mythology. What do we do if Saturnalia really is the one true god? Or Isis? It becomes endless, and irrelevant.

3) Say it's all the same God, with different rules. You get judged by the standards you were told about. For you and me, that's Christianity. For a Muslim, that's the Quran. "What rules were you told about? Did you hear about the punishments? Did you follow the rules? No? Why shouldn't you be punished?

Answer: Say an orange is actually a pencil. Can you write with it now? The different views of various supernatural entities are completely incompatible (like oranges and pencils...). But even if you're right, by your logic I'm still OK. My "god" in this context is a search for truth in the context of logic. And in that context, for me to have come to any other conclusion would have been to ignore the rules I have been taught, and thus face eternal consequences.

19 ABSOLUTES AND MEANING

January 22nd, 2014:

This is the 19th installment in my deconversion series of posts. In the morality miniseries, an oft-asked but off-topic question was "how can you call anything moral if there is no ultimate moral standard?" In this post, I address that question, as well as the broader question of ultimate meaning and purpose in a naturalist, Humanist worldview.

****

Ultimates: Right and Wrong, Purpose, and Meaning

In the beginning of the morality miniseries, I laid out a naturalist basis that explains why morality has improved as time has passed - a kind of cultural evolution via natural selection. I was not attempting to define ultimate morality, but rather explain why we observed what we consider to be moral behavior in human interactions. For some, however, the question of "but why do we call this moral and not other things?" leads to a conclusion that somewhere out there must be an ultimate standard of morality, and thus an ultimate moral law giver. This turns out to be a completely unnecessary conclusion.

Let's clear the air just a bit: If morality is determined, as I propose, by long-term advantage gained via repeated cultural exchanges, then it's not really morality by any objective, ultimate standard. It's intelligently applied selfish behavior. And yes, I agree with that 100%, and would thus say there is no such thing as ultimate morality. That's not to say that all behaviors are thus equally valid. The straw man of "the serial killer is no less objectively moral than the saint" is quickly thrown out based on cultural evolution. Our laws codify those behaviors that we believe - either consciously or unconsciously - produce the best overall outcomes for our society. If we were to allow wanton murder, our society would devolve into a dangerous place with high transaction costs. Thus, we penalize those who engage in such behaviors to protect our society. You don't need an ultimate moral standard to come to the conclusion that these very unequal transactions (one person gains satisfaction, the other person loses their life) should not be allowed for the overall good. This is also why, as our understanding of the Platinum Rule improves over time, other behaviors that were once seen as immoral must be redefined and accepted. Homophobia, racism, and gender discrimination come to mind here.

Furthermore, morality is relative in nearly all cases anyway. Nearly any action is considered good or bad based on the circumstances and cultural environment. Killing is bad, unless you're defending your children from a murderer and there's no other alternative to stop them. Praising a child's behavior is good, unless that child just did something terribly wrong, in which case the praise becomes evil. Nearly any action falls into the category of relative morality. Even historical context matters - the Old Testament law forbade mercy in many, many contexts[54], but New Testament examples implied it was necessary in nearly all contexts[55]. The examples here can go on and on, but the end conclusion remains - morality is relative, and based largely on context and a recognition of overall societal consequences and advantage. There is no absolute moral standard, just what works best if everyone engaged in it. Thus, we have the Platinum Rule…

Let's push this idea further. Another criticism of naturalism is that it's reductionist and removes any sense of ultimate meaning or purpose from our lives. In one sense, I agree with that statement. If we really are just a collection of atoms with no supernatural component, if there is no ultimate morality, and if someday our ultimate destiny as a race is simply to die out as our planet and/or our universe eventually runs out of livable space, then from a long-term view, our actions have no ultimate meaning. That said, I am not a Nihilist. I do not believe that the absence of "ultimate" meaning means that we cannot discover relative meaning in the life experience we are granted. In fact, I see humanity and the emergence of sentient life as being an amazing opportunity with a world of possibilities to explore. We are free to choose, in the time we have, our own moments of purpose, meaning, and significance, and there is no ultimately wrong answer! It's like winning a lottery and being handed a blank check - the possibilities are

---

[54] See Deuteronomy 25:11-12
[55] See John 8:7

limitless! Those who choose to view the lack of ultimate meaning in a spirit of doom and gloom are seriously missing the boat. It's that same lottery winner who realizes that they cannot possibly do everything in the world before they die, and so they tear up the check out of disgust. How ridiculous would that be? In fact, acknowledging the reality of relative morality can lead to a greater awareness of this gift of life on this earth and help us avoid surrendering the many wonderful opportunities it brings us (as long as the Platinum Rule is observed) in exchange for some nonexistent heavenly reward. As one of my friends commented: You only get to go around once, so make the most of it! I couldn't agree more.

****

Again, it was an agnostic friend that had the most insightful comments in response to this post.

> 1) Those who think their own morality comes from God end up realizing that any initial rush that their misbehavior that resulted from giving up that belief would quickly be overwhelmed by their own inner sense of guilt and shame.
>
> Answer: Good point. My primary goal in *this* post was not to explain why we observe moral behavior. Instead, here I simply discuss whether absolutes exist and the ramifications and misconceptions if they don't. And as you point out, in the final analysis their lack of existence does not fundamentally change most human behavior, particularly in those with the capacity to appreciate the long-term consequences of their decisions. Sure, there are some throughout history who have decided as a result of denying faith that they would take on a hedonist, objectivist, or nihilist world view. I think they're crazy, and that evidence points to that not ending well in most cases, which is why Humanism makes a lot of sense to me. However, those same examples have equally evil, if not more evil, parallels in human history where a Christian religious framework was used to justify horrors and atrocities. Human beings are human beings, and not everyone thinks through issues correctly or comes to the right conclusions, but those who claim "atheism necessarily leads to x" (x being a bad thing) are making serious errors in their analysis. It may be true in some cases, but that is also true of Christianity and most other world religions.

20 ATHEIST RELIGION

January 23rd, 2014:

> This is the 20th installment in my deconversion series of posts. In this post I examine the question of whether religion or religious constructs can have any value for an atheist. It's a pragmatic question - religions are going to be around for a long time, and while I think atheists have a right to push for truth-based systems of belief and that they are superior overall, in the interim does that mean we have to rail against any and all things with religious overtones? Not at all, and where religion has value in our world today, until atheists have reasonable replacements, it is likely in our best interests to use them for what they are good for. (Christian friends frustrated by my coming out may well enjoy the negative atheist onslaught coming my way in response to this article. My fireproof underpants are in place...)

****

Is There Value in Religion for Atheists?

Can value be had from belief in Christianity or other religions, even if those beliefs are not true? While I ultimately believe a world that embraces truth is the best-case scenario, I am also a realist and understand that religion and religious people are going to be around for a long time. Thus, I try to find whatever common ground I can with folks who disagree with me on the supernatural question, and even as an atheist, I can find value in religious constructs.

The first and most important value for me is in my immediate family. I have already written of the value I see in my daughter's Christian school and its more intensive focus on morality than a public school would provide. I have also often-stated, but not clarified in this context, that I say bedtime prayers with my son and support his belief in God. This puzzles some of my atheist friends (and puts some of them up in arms), but the best way I can explain why I do this is what I call the Santa Claus effect. Little children are often taught to believe in an all-knowing being who rewards good behavior with presents on Christmas day. This is often used to help small children make better behavioral decisions than they otherwise might - at least for a few weeks every year. My 9-year-old son has autism. One of the challenges of autism is a certain blindness to how others are affected by his behavior, which makes application of the Platinum Rule challenging in any "in the moment" situation. For him, a rules-based approach to morality is simply more effective and helps him make better decisions today than my attempts to instill a Platinum Rule-based decision mechanism have been. As such, I continue to support that rules-based Christian worldview while I wait for his abilities to grow to the point where the rules crutch is no longer necessary and he is able to process the effects of his behaviors on others in real time. This principle can hold true for typically developing children as well, as long as it's used while attempting to instill the others-based Platinum Rule framework.

The second value I see in Christianity, in particular, is the inaccurate view (in my opinion) that the Bible portrays Jesus as the ideal man. Miles Kimball, a Mormon-turned-atheist and professor of economics, wrote an amazing post in which he outlines the social value of humans first picturing some kind of moral ideal and then trying to follow it - however imperfectly - in their own lives.

http://blog.supplysideliberal.com/post/56663457380/godless-religion

In my own life, I taught myself how to be a father and husband despite a lack of good examples at home in part by imagining God/Jesus as the perfect role model and working as hard as I could to develop personality traits to match what I thought he would do in any given situation. That exercise proved to be of tremendous value in my marriage and my family relationships.

The third value I see in religion is in giving a framework of meaning and morality - although imperfect in many ways - to folks who lack the emotional ability or straight-up intelligence to be able to think through and deal with life's issues on their own. (I am NOT saying this applies to everyone, or even the majority of religious people today.) There is actually a body of research that seems to indicate that for some people religious beliefs help counteract depressive tendencies. This, in part, is why I am not in any hurry to obliterate all religion, but would rather see it phased out and minimized over time. I think the cost of losing one's foundations without the ability to reconstruct a new one might be too high for some to pay.

The final value I see in religion is in the social constructs it provides. Religious folks have a common set of ideals and values that can easily transport from one community to another. Regular religious services provide a framework for social interaction, self improvement-focused education, and community activism that atheists by and large have not found a way to meaningfully replace. To be sure, there are instances of individual success stories I have learned about via TCP. Jerry DeWitt has done some great work with his Community Mission Chapel[56]. The Houston Oasis[57] is another great example. One United Church of Canada minister, Gretta Vosper, actually came out of the closet as an atheist and rather than fire her, her church chose to walk down that road with her![58] (This is by far the exception rather than the rule.) That said, these are individual bright spots in an otherwise barren landscape for secular "religious" communities. There are some coordinated, top-down movements afoot - the one I am most excited about is the Sunday Assembly[59] - to replicate all of those good things that organized religion can provide without the religious beliefs attached. I am hopeful that in a few years, atheists will have the same opportunities to join together, sing songs that move them, examine and improve themselves, and generally enjoy community with one another just like Christians do today. Until that time, being part of a religious community can have value even if one doesn't believe.

This is not meant to be interpreted as a support for organized religion. It is simply an acknowledgement that nonbelievers have some things to learn from believers, and working towards organizing around these issues and challenges will go a long way towards moving atheism - and specifically, atheist religion - into the mainstream.

****

---

[56] https://www.facebook.com/CommunityMissionChapel
[57] http://www.houstonoasis.org/wp/
[58] http://www.grettavosper.ca/about/
[59] http://sundayassembly.com/

While some atheists disagreed with me on the value of religion to them, they did acknowledge that others might find value in those things. Hopefully movements like The Sunday Assembly and similar, along with more progressive Christian movements, will make it possible to replicate what is good in religion without the supernatural clutter.

21 THE 10 COMMITMENTS

January 24th, 2014 (morning):

> This is the 21st installment in my deconversion series of posts. In my last post I pointed out that there was value for some in a rules-based religious construct and that atheists haven't yet developed an infrastructure to replace what is good about that. I received a couple of questions as to what I would propose as a starting place for building on such an infrastructure, and one person specifically pointed to the 10 Commandments (in addition to the Golden Rule) as that basis for Christianity. Thus, I present to you an initial stab at the "10 Commitments" which aims to codify the Platinum Rule for atheists, Humanists, Freethinkers, and other folks who, like me, believe in a solely natural world.

****

The 10 Commitments
(based on the Platinum Rule)

1) I will not believe in gods or supernatural forces without objective evidence of their existence.

2) I will remember that most of my views and opinions are based on imperfect and incomplete information, and as new and better data become available, I will modify those opinions and views accordingly.

3) I will treat all humans with respect without regard to race, gender, sexual orientation, age, celebrity status, profession, social status, education level,

financial status, disability, level of agreement or disagreement with my views on any issue, or any other element that differentiates us as human beings.

4) I will raise my children, to the extent of their own ability, to think for themselves, examine available evidence, and come to their own conclusions based on logic, reason, and data.

5) I will take care of my body (including proper eating, exercise, and rest), my health (including behavioral habits and proper medical care), and my emotional well-being (including relationships I engage in and influences I choose to allow in my life).

6) I will honor agreements I make and deal fairly with others in all relationships. This includes marriages, friendships, casual exchanges, and business/professional relationships.

7) I will set aside time to spend with friends, family, and other loved ones and pay attention to the meaning and value they build into my life.

8) I will be careful in both action and language and ensure to the greatest degree possible that I never use my abilities to harm others.

9) I will use my time, abilities, and financial resources to support causes that help move humanity in a positive direction.

10) I will be a good citizen of the world and will take care of my family, my community, my country, and my planet.

****

I followed up this post with the following comments:

> Just like Christians and the 10 Commandments, there are some of these that I don't personally follow as well as others in my own life - in particular, the 5th commitment with regards to taking care of my body. I'm working on it though, and since these are commitments rather than commandments, there is more freedom to use them as a guide rather than a driving force. There's freedom to fail without fear.
>
> These ideas are also captured extremely well in the Humanist Manifesto III:
>
> http://americanhumanist.org/Humanism/Humanist_Manifesto_III

I got one question from a fellow atheist about whether I should have included something about happiness, awe, and wonder in life for ourselves and others. I had actually considered that, but I finally came down on those being the end-results of obeying the Platinum Rule rather than actionable items within it. If I ever do an "Atheist Beatitudes," that's probably where those kind of ideas would fit.

Otherwise, there was little conversation on this post. I didn't really expect a lot, as these codify the kind of morality I think most Christians would like to think of themselves as keeping to (with exception for the first, and maybe second commitments).

22 DEATH AND JUSTICE

January 24th, 2014 (afternoon):

This is the 22nd installment in my deconversion series of posts, my second one for today. This one addresses another couple of heartfelt questions I have received during my coming out journey: What do I think happens when we die, and what about justice? This also addresses why my non-supernatural worldview provides greater peace than my Christian beliefs did, as well as why I have a sense of urgency for making sure we build our world the right way in the time we have on this planet.

****

What Happens When We Die? What About Justice?

What Happens When We Die?

This one is very close to the hearts of a lot of folks, many of whom I think ask it because they may be afraid I'm right. When we breathe our last, what next? We want to believe we will see loved ones who have died again someday. For many, this is a source of comfort, and a question I hesitate to answer for that very reason.

But, it comes up - a lot - and so here goes.

I believe when we die, we fall asleep one last time and simply never wake up. Our consciousness ceases to exist. Our world ends. The closest thing I have experienced to what I think this is like is deep sleep. You probably know what it feels like to close your eyes and open them hours later without having been conscious of any time passing. I think that's what death is like, sort of. It's not "eternal blackness" or some other such horrible sounding thing. Being aware of eternal blackness requires consciousness, which, if we're biological beings and that's all, does not exist once our brains shut down. It's simply non-existence. It's the same thing you and I experienced (if you can call it that) before being born.

At first I will admit the thought of non-existence was terrifying, but now it's actually comforting. Eternity can be a terrifying concept if you really think about it, even if you think it's going to be pleasant. In addition, with my previous worldview, too many really well meaning people that I had grown to love were going to eternal torture because they believed the wrong things, had the wrong genetic makeup, grew up in the wrong families, lived in the wrong parts of the world, etc. Given the two alternatives, I can be happy with a final rest.

This belief also makes me value time and relationships with loved ones now even more. Yes, I would still love to believe in an afterlife where I get to spend eternity with loved ones. Wanting something to be true doesn't make it so. Hope is not a life strategy. Thus, I make sure and squeeze every ounce of joy I can out of the time I have with folks now, and think fondly of those who have gone on for their final rest.

What About Justice?

Final rest can be comforting when we think about loved ones in pain, but what about the bad guys? What about Hitler? Does he deserve rest? Wouldn't we all like to think he's merrily being roasted by a horde of demons in torture and agony?

Well, if it makes you feel better, continue with the visualization. However, wishing something were true does not make it so. Something is either true or it's not, and what I or we want to be true will not change what is. You might also be careful what you wish for. For many of my religious friends, there is little to no difference between Hitler's eternal fate and my good friend who grew up in a loving Hindu family and values all paths to "truth" in whatever form. If it's a matter of "want" to believe, I would rather believe Hitler found an easy way out than to believe my Hindu friend burns for eternity. Given no credible evidence for the existence of an afterlife in any form, there's no reason to worry. When she dies, her world ends, just like Hitler's did.

As far as overall justice then, my belief also makes me more adamant about seeking justice during life, just as it drives me to spend time with loved ones on a regular basis. It's more important for me to do something now, while I still have breath, because I know there isn't going to be some supernatural payday in either direction.

This is the one life we have, we are extremely fortunate to be living it, and we should make the most of it in every way we can. That focused awareness is one of the many gifts of atheism.

****

This post generated a significant response, in particular around the subject of suicide, and specifically doctor-assisted suicide. I ended up deflecting what I consider to be extremism on both sides of the issue.

1) Doesn't this post make the case for suicide and euthanasia?

Answer: Only if you've disregarded everything I've said up to this point. If life is short and has a termination point, it is extremely valuable and precious. Suicide under most circumstances (with exceptions for things like jumping on a grenade to save your friends, etc.) violates the Platinum Rule in a large number of ways.

End of life cycle euthanasia on the other hand, I will absolutely agree, is a tougher subject, and one which neither Humanism nor Christianity provides a clear answer that would apply in all situations. The one thing that Humanism gives me that I didn't have as a Christian is the ability to say "there is no right answer that applies to all situations." Ending a life for medical mercy reasons to end suffering that serves no purpose is a serious consideration, but if it turns out to be the most loving, caring thing to do, the Platinum Rule (and most other moral codes) should allow for it. Again though, I don't say that as though it's a flippant, easy decision. It's just that I don't believe it to be moral to cut it off as an option in all situations.

2) But what ensures that those who are struggling with really difficult life circumstances are violating the Platinum Rule by allowing themselves eternal rest from the struggles around them? And again, since all things are relative, you do hold life to be valuable, but not everyone agrees on that at all.

Answer: You've said nothing I disagree with, other than "not everyone agrees on that..." as though someone's opinion that life is not valuable should merit equal weight in the discussion. It doesn't, because life and human experience can be objectively, quantifiably shown to have tremendous worth. Calling a Nihilist on their world views is the duty of a Humanist like me.

As far as many - if not most - situations are concerned, I am sure most people have amazing reasons to continue living: loved ones, friends, more life to experience, more to share, etc. However, there are darker examples where this is not as clear. Scott Adams, the creator of the Dilbert cartoon series, wrote a post that described his personal situation, one in which I would struggle to make such an easy call. (Warning, strong language and very, very raw emotions expressed...)

http://www.dilbert.com/blog/entry/i_hope_my_father_dies_soon/

3) Your belief as a Humanist that life is valuable does not change the fact that there are a LOT of people who do not feel that way about their own lives. Their families have abandoned them. They are in deep debt. They don't have good jobs. They don't have significant others. Any one of those things can cause a person to feel like life is not valuable. How do you convince them that it is? And why would you want to? What is the point of trying to get them to stick around if it would be easier for them to rest?

Answer: The short answer is "potential." Those who have been abandoned and struggle with all of those things can choose to continue to live lives that have value for themselves and for others around them. If they have given up on this, I would gently remind them of the value they can have to whomever they choose to come in contact with, directly or indirectly. Feeling like life is bleak is not equivalent to having a bleak life.

An illustration I think helps me clarify the point in my mind: In *Last of the Mohicans* (the movie) I vividly remember a scene where one of the characters in the movie is being burned at the stake. The hero of the movie gets to a safe distance and then turns around and shoots the man. Is this immoral? No. He had no options: no path available, no life worth living ahead of him. He was going to die; it was just a matter of speed, and that was all that was left in his life. Putting him out of

91

his misery was infinitely more moral than allowing him to fully experience the flames that would torture him to the end of his life anyway. Would you disagree?

I look at the euthanasia issue in much the same way. Yes, there are going to be gray area cases, but there are many, many cases where there is no gray area, and forcing a person's body to go on living despite their condition is - as Scott Adams said - nothing short of torture. In those cases, I believe the individual, their doctors, and their families should be able to make the choice to end the person's suffering. I believe to do otherwise in those specific (and carefully selected/evaluated) cases is immoral.

If you disagree, then what you are probably saying is that you believe the hero of the movie should have let the man experience the fullness of the agonies in being burned at the stake. My moral code doesn't allow me to believe that is true.

Here's the scene to which I'm referring - the first two minutes is all you need to watch. Not fun, but does bring this point home.

https://www.youtube.com/watch?v=ah9XCamPyKA

4) Should we as a society or individual have the right to prevent another individual from making the choice to die in a manner in a time and place that he or she chooses? How can one even argue that a person is free or has freedom when he or she does not even have a right to make decisions regarding his or her own life?

Answer: You go further than what I am willing to go at this point in my journey, because sometimes I wonder if humans shouldn't be protected from themselves in a moment of weakness. Consider a man who might have elected suicide when learning he had Parkinson's, which in my view today might not be a good enough justification for doctor-assisted suicide. This is one of those issues where none of the "easy" answers sit well with me as I evaluate them based on all of the variables. The particulars of each situation would make it such that I would want to be very, very careful in application. Someone's desire to die at any given moment may well not be enough justification to allow medical professionals to enable that wish. The entire situation would need to be considered rather than that single point of data.

92

5) What concerns me is that who is defining the moment of weakness we are protecting someone from? I personally would not want to continue to live if my life was of such a poor quality that I could no longer enjoy the experience, and I were to have to spend the remainder of my life in a drug induced haze in order to be able to partially dull constant physical pain. This type of life would not be living but merely existing.

Answer: I think that you can craft guidelines for how such a decision might be made. For example, in my teens I contemplated suicide (for various reasons). I lacked perspective, and to have had professional assistance to enable my wish would have been tragic. I'm not saying that I know exactly what those guidelines should be in all cases, and readily admit this is a tough situation to consider, but I still think there are clear situations where it is the right thing to do (i.e. something equivalent to the guy in the movie clip) and clear situations where it is the wrong thing to do (i.e. a depressed teenager). It is sometimes the right thing to do to ignore one's wishes, if and when a clear understanding of their ramifications violates a moral principle. Or so I believe. Sometimes a human's life is more valuable than that human realizes, and they should at least be given time and opportunity (counseling, etc.) to gain perspective before making such a decision.

6) I have to admit, as an atheist not believing in an afterlife makes euthanasia seem much more reasonable. I am challenged by this.

Answer: I'm really curious about this, because frankly my beliefs went the other way. Prior to becoming an atheist, the end of life here was just a beginning of the next life, and so I was more favorable towards euthanasia to end the suffering of believers than I am today. When this is the only life we have, I think we have to treat the subject more carefully and weigh the potential value of whatever life is left more heavily than we do if we are allowed to take an eternal worldview. Interesting that your experience took you in the opposite direction.

7) If atheists are correct in their view, they are not very moral as a whole. If they believe that justice must come in this world or be denied forever, then they should be working harder as a group to fight injustice. As it stands, many if not most atheists seem to be myopically selfish, mainly focused on enjoying their own lives and less concerned

about injustice. Without God, there appears to be no way to persuade them to care about those suffering.

Answer: You have highlighted one of the reasons I have gone to great lengths in my coming out journey to detail Humanist morality and why I believe it is a superior atheist view. It is true that many atheists are Hedonists, and others Nihilists, and while I understand how they got to that viewpoint, I believe they hurt themselves in the long run. I also think they collectively make it easier for society to dismiss them and hinder the ability of atheists in general to engage in social dialog. Frankly, I think the fact that such a small percentage of folks worldwide are atheists today is one of the consequences of these worldviews broadly being attributed to atheism. As I pointed out in my very first morality miniseries post, natural selection via the Nash Equilibrium dictates that those who engage in selfish behaviors over repeated transactions will be in large part marginalized (if not neutralized) in a society that is culturally moral. The fact that most people consider their religion to be morally superior to their conception of atheist worldviews goes a long way towards explaining why people in general have such visceral reactions to atheists regardless of context.

I am coming out as an atheist, but just as importantly, a Humanist - not because I necessarily want to be seen as a moral person (although I do), but because I would have followed the data wherever it led. I am a Humanist because I believe it is the correct view to hold given all of the data. Hedonism and Nihilism are not consistent with optimal long-term outcomes given our best available information, and thus I reject them. It is my hope that atheists who follow my journey will also be able to see the potential error in their ways if applicable, and make corrections that benefit themselves and all humankind in the long run.

I was beginning to realize just how important the Humanist label was going to be moving forward. Atheism has potentially bad philosophies if one is lazy, selfish, or uninformed. I had been a critic of fundamentalism as a believer, I realized I would have to be equally critical of atheists who through either thinking errors or just plain selfishness refused to recognize the prime importance of the Platinum Rule. I have resigned myself to the fact that I am never going to win a popularity contest.

23 THE PRICE OF AUTHENTICITY

January 25th, 2014:

This is the 23rd - and final - installment in my deconversion series of posts. It's been a long and interesting journey, and I want to thank everyone who stuck it out, who challenged my ideas, and who supported me through every post. I may do additional writing if people ask additional questions (or remind me of a topic I forgot to cover) but this is the last of the official posts in the deconversion series.

Someone asked a very poignant question very early on in the series: Why does it matter what I believe, or that other people know that I believe what I believe? I had a good thing going when everyone thought I was a Christian, so what on earth could make it worth the pain to go public as an atheist / Humanist? Surely I could have made it through another few decades of life pretending to believe a beautiful lie? This post takes that question head-on and explains why I could not just remain silent.

I ended my series with a post I had actually written long before, when I was trying to decide whether to go public with my beliefs or not. You'll also recognize it as being very similar to the preface of the book.

****

Being Authentic, and Why Most People Aren't

What if being honest meant losing things that were dear to you?

- Your job?
- Your standing in the community?
- Your friendships?
- Your family relationships?
- Your marriage?

Would you have the ability to maintain a lie if you thought it was mostly harmless in order to keep these things in your life in place? I suspect many of you reading this already do. Some of you reject the authority of the Bible as I do, for the same reasons, but still publicly claim that it is the "inspired word of God" and only hope that no one notices the crazy stuff and calls you on it.

The question is, at what point of harm does a lie become too great to maintain, regardless of the cost? At what point does bigotry against homosexuals, women, and people of other nations become untenable for you, even if it is endorsed by your holy writings? At what point does the unconscionable act of lying about science in order to indoctrinate your children start to cause real harm both to them and to the scientific progress potential of humanity in general? At what point does the money spent on lavish cathedrals, massive salaries, enormous mansions, and private jets for ministers and their self-serving ministries start to weigh on your conscience when children around the world die every day from lack of food, water, and basic sanitation? At what point should people who refuse or delay medical treatment for their sick children based on "the power of prayer" - which has been proven time and time again to be ineffective - lose the right to make those decisions for their kids?

If belief in the supernatural were truly harmless, I'd have no problem maintaining the lie. Unfortunately, believing a lie is never really truly harmless. It affects decisions as small as a hiring manager choosing a lesser-qualified candidate based on bigotry to as large as a national leader believing we are living in the end times and seeing himself as a fulfillment of some apocalyptic prophecy. Truth, it turns out, and can be the difference between life and death in both direct and indirect ways.

For many of us embedded in our religious communities, however, the cost of saying "the emperor has no clothes" comes at a steep price. Full-time clergy or religious business leaders who have come to the realization that their faith is a sham risk financial hardship for their families if they come clean to their followers or customers. Religious people in the community will almost certainly talk about "that poor family with the atheist mom/dad" and put them on various prayer lists (gossip chains). If most of your friendships, family relationships, and even your marriage are based on a common set of beliefs, you risk losing it all. I have personally observed that the divorce rate for clergy who dare speak honestly about their doubts or lack of faith is amazingly high, with marriage survival seeming to be the exception rather than the rule. All of this is based on an attempt to be an honest, authentic human being. It breaks my heart.

Thus, I have a lot of sympathy for those of you who can't let yourselves follow truth wherever it leads. I get the struggle. I understand the potential social costs and the nearly certain loss of important relationships. If this is you, I do not ask you to follow me on my public truth journey - not yet. The challenge I have for you is to find ways to help those of us for whom the cost of living a lie has become too high. Continue being our friends and lean into that relationship just a little bit more. Be a listening ear and a shoulder to cry on. Be a place of refuge in our lives. Perhaps consider direct financial assistance if the situation calls for it. Support us (even if just privately) in our fight for truth and honesty, because in the end, we're fighting for your right to be honest with the world about who you really are as well.

Someday, maybe, you'll get to add your voice to the growing chorus of doubt or even all-out nonbelief without fear of losing those things that matter most. That, friends, is why my journey matters to more than just me, and why I - full knowing the social cost - stepped out on a limb and made my views and their reasons public. I was either going to be shown the error of my ways (which did not happen) or provide light on a path that others might follow when they're ready and able to do so. I support you, even if I don't know who you are, and will help you in any way I can if and when you decide to come out of the closet for yourself.

As a dear friend and the person I consider to be my atheist big brother told me when I first went public with my changed views: "Welcome out of the cave. It's colder out here, but the stars are beautiful."

He did not lie.

****

The conversation that followed included reminders from Christians that I'd know for sure when I died whether I was right or not, expressions of gratitude for promoting critical thought, and some continued discussion on various topics of morality. This included an extended conversation between me and another atheist around the use of violence and what kinds of means justify the use of violence.

Folks got to witness my Platinum Rule-based morality challenged by an "ends justify the means" moral stance where any action could be justified if it alleviated overall suffering. The contents of that debate could make up an entire booklet all its own. Suffice it to say, his conviction was based on a belief that those with the ability to inflict violence on others would be in agreement with his worldview - a view I thought to be optimistic at best. My conviction included a sincere hope that natural selection would eventually weed out his line of thought from all humanity. I won't say it was a fun discussion, but I was glad that the Christians in my Friends list got to see me duke it out with what I would characterize as a fundamentalist on the other side of the fence.

I will finish with a loose quote from one of my comments:

> I think atheism is going through an evolution, just like Christianity did from the Old to New Testament. The end results of the Nash Equilibrium have only been studied for a few years, so in times past atheists did not have a construct for Humanism other than a gut feeling that it was the right thing to do. Thus many atheists became Hedonists or Nihilists.

> I'm looking down the road, and I see much greater opportunities for Humanists ahead. I welcome any and all - believers or nonbelievers - to join me in the quest to optimize the potential of all humankind.

EPILOGUE

So now what?

I did not set out to make this into a book. I expected to write about 8 or 9 posts and then move on with my life. Little did I imagine the number of great questions that would be raised, nor the level of interest folks would have in my story. As I found the number of topics multiplying and the coming out party becoming a multi-week affair, I had several friends who encouraged me to put this in print and make it available to a larger audience. They thought it might make a difference. And so I did.

I have also been approached by many friends - a few of whom proclaimed their own lack of belief in the supernatural in public for the first time, and many, many others who for family or community / cultural reasons must remain in the closet for now. All of them have expressed their gratitude and several specifically made it known that they would love to have the writings as a resource to give to family and friends. For what purpose I can only imagine - to challenge them, perhaps to open the door to a hard conversation? I can only imagine the reasons are as varied as the individuals who asked. This book exists for them as well.

A third group of interested individuals was perhaps the most intriguing of all: believers. One of the things my believing friends said they appreciated about my writing is that I was a departure from the "angry atheist" stereotype that seems to dominate a lot of public discourse. I believe thoughtful books that respect the viewpoints of those who disagree need to be out there, and I was told my writings strike a good balance between confronting someone on their views while still respecting them as individuals. Mine is not the first book like this, and it will certainly not be the last, but having more of them out there is better than fewer, and I'm happy to be part of that movement.

That said, I must say that I have a tremendous amount of respect for all of the well-known individuals that defend a naturalist worldview, even if I don't believe the approaches many of them take are the most productive for getting people to consider their views. Many revolutions start with wars by necessity, and if the early atheist warriors had been nice guys (wimps) like me, odds are I would not live in a time where the biggest thing I have to worry about is losing some friends and dealing with minor hassles in my community. I am certainly not the first voice of tolerance, nor will I be the last, but I still have a great amount of admiration for those who fought because they had to who made it possible for me to be myself without significant fear. I owe them a lot.

But I'm still dodging the question. What now? Many folks have pointed out that my short essays could each use a more thorough treatment and better overall organization by topic rather than by day posted. Nearly every topic could benefit from more in-depth research details, and there are many additional topics that could be discussed that simply never came up in this conversation. Some suggested that I could create some kind of YouTube channel, blog, or web site where links would be easier to use and reference. I would enjoy writing a more detailed book of science and apologia in my specific style of speech and presentation, if enough public interest was there to do so. If not, I'm happy to let this be my final printed words on these subjects. If I'm honest, nearly anything I could say has been said, more thoroughly, eloquently, and with more authority than I could muster on most topics. If I have anything to add, it is simply being another voice in a growing chorus.

In the end though, my main goal of writing any of this down, and then putting it into a book form, was to get you to think. Do I believe most people will be persuaded by my reasoning? No, not most. There will be a few, most of whom were probably already questioning but hadn't yet found the answers they needed to commit to a naturalist worldview. If that's you, I'm glad you found the book and I hope it helped point you in the right direction. If I had any major goal, however, it was to show people that someone like Jason Eden could become an honest atheist. I'm a nice guy, for better or worse. I love my wife and children dearly. I deeply understand the Bible. I can laugh at myself, and frankly, I give myself a lot of opportunities to do so. It's easier to be dogmatic when you can dehumanize "them" vs. "us", but if you're a Christian fundamentalist, I was just like you at one point, with the same views, feelings, and fears. If I've made atheists real human beings for you, made it harder to lump them all together in some category that you have permission to despise with impunity, then I have accomplished everything I set out to do.

This book is finished, but it is only the beginning of what promises to be an amazing journey. Won't you join me?

ABOUT THE AUTHOR

Jason Eden is a husband of a loving, patient woman and the father of two children who serve as consistent reminders of the need for grace (with a lower-case g) for all of humanity, but also serve to remind him of the amazing power of human potential that sometimes hides beneath the surface. He is a Humanist Celebrant endorsed by the Humanist Society and a member of The Clergy Project. Professionally he works in corporate education, typically with software companies in either training, course development, eLearning, or certification capacities. He is the author of **Staging A Miracle - A Practical Parent's Guide to Surviving an Autism Diagnosis**, which is available in paperback on Amazon, as well as in digital form for Kindle or Nook devices.

He can be reached via email at
JasonEden@MidwestHumanist.com.

Made in the USA
San Bernardino, CA
18 May 2014